Healing the Wounds

Healing the Wounds

One Family's Journey Among the Northern Cheyenne

Poetry by Ann Wenger

Prose by Esther and Malcolm Wenger

National Library of Canada Cataloguing in Publication Data

Wenger, Ann
    Healing the wounds: One Family's Journey Among the Northern Cheyenne

ISBN 1-894710-09-6

1. Children of missionaries – Montana – Poetry. 2. Mennonites – Missions –
Montana – Poetry. 3. Cheyenne Indians – Missions – Montana – Poetry.
4. Missionaries – Montana. 5. Mennonites – Missions – Montana.
6. Cheyenne Indians – Missions – Montana. I. Wenger, Esther. II. Wenger,
Malcolm. III. Title.

PS3623.E53H42 2001   811'.6   C2001-930760-8

HEALING THE WOUNDS:
ONE FAMILY'S JOURNEY AMONG THE NORTHERN CHEYENNE
Copyright © 2001 by Pandora Press
33 Kent Avenue
Kitchener, Ontario, N2G 3R2
www.pandorapress.com
All rights reserved.

Copublished with Herald Press,
Scottdale, Pennsylvania/Waterloo, Ontario

International Standard Book Number: 1-894710-09-6
Printed in Canada on acid-free paper.

Cover and book design by Clifford Snyder
Cover illustration by Ann Wenger

10 09 08 07 06 05 04 03 02 01   12 11 10 9 8 7 6 5 4 3 2 1

Table of Contents

Introduction

This book grew out of the experiences of a girl caught between two very different worlds—the German Mennonite world of her parents, and the world of the Northern Cheyenne people to whom her parents had come as missionaries. Children of missionaries learn from their playmates as well as their parents. This girl absorbed the richness as well as the pain of the Cheyenne experience.

That girl, that woman, is our daughter, Ann. But there were shadows in Ann's life that we did not fully understand—shadows she dealt with by writing poetry. Many years later, she asked us to wrap her poems in prose that would reveal our thoughts, feelings and reactions to the same experiences and give some context to the haunting memories that gave birth to the poems. "These words are not about Indian people as such," she says, "they are my story behind the mission station. They do not express the way things were, but the way I felt about the way things were. These words are not about facts; they are about being."

Back: Esther, Rebecca, Malcolm. Front: Ann, Elizabeth, Lillian Whistlingelk, neighbor girl.

The poems and stories are based on events of the 1940s, '50s and '60s on the Northern Cheyenne reservation in Montana, together with later experiences among other First Nation peoples and the Metis of Canada. We have learned much from these brothers and

1

Ann and her sister Elizabeth sitting on mission home porch.

sisters. Not having kept a diary or journal apart from letters we wrote to our families, we rely heavily on memory. And we acknowledge the frailties of that memory. The stories we remember, of course, are those that caught our attention, that taught us something. Others will, no doubt, remember the same events differently, and we would welcome their stories and memories.

We adults often shielded ourselves from the pain of the Cheyenne community around us by a kind of clinical detachment. With so many funerals, how could we weep at each one? Our daughter Ann was more able to take within herself the struggle of the whole people; to feel it, to weep over it. Working as a teenager in the local store, she saw hungry people ask for food and had to say "no." It was Ann who brought us the news that a young mother, Beverly, a sister in the Lord, had leaned her chin on the muzzle of a deer rifle and pushed the trigger—no longer able to accept her husband's unfaithfulness.

We, Ann's parents, hope that sharing our feelings, thoughts and experiences will not only complement her poetry but will be a healing touch to those who lived through these events, painful though some of them were. May each reader find some understanding that God can use in their life.

While Esther and I worked closely together on this project, I, Malcolm, narrate the stories that follow. We have assumed that the "real" names of the people whose stories are included here are their Cheyenne names. So we have used direct translations of these names into English, although these are not the names these people go by in English. Some names have been changed.

—*Esther and Malcolm Wenger*

Foreword

Take the Savior as Your Friend

Take the Savior as your friend!
His way alone is good.
His story alone is true.
It has spread all over the world!
—*Nova'keso* (Slow Growing Woman),
Newakis Lamebull[1]

And this gospel of the kingdom
will be preached in the whole world
as a testimony to all nations....
Matthew 24:14[2]

How We Got Involved

I learned my first words of Cheyenne from Slow Growing Woman, or Newakis Lamebull as we called her in English. At the time I had no inkling that the rest of my life would be entwined with the *Tsetsestase*, the Cheyenne people. I was studying languages at the Summer Institute of Linguistics in Muskogee, Oklahoma. Slow Growing Woman and people of other Native American tribes were there to help train us by speaking to us in languages entirely unrelated to the Indo-European French, German or Spanish usually offered in colleges. Sampling the "exotic" sounds and the "strange" grammars of languages such as Oto, Commanche, Kiowa and Cheyenne was to better prepare us to learn unwritten languages well enough to translate into them.

Slow Growing Woman had helped train Bible translators who were already at work in distant places. Letters from her former students inspired a song composed in Cheyenne which translates as "Take the Savior as Your Friend!"

I, too, felt drawn to the task of taking Jesus' good news to the world. My home church had planted some of this desire in me. A former Sunday School teacher once told me that already as a young boy, if asked what I wanted to be when I grew up, I would answer, "a missionary."

Currents moving through the larger Mennonite world washed over our Aberdeen, Idaho, congregation as well. After years of persecution, and then many years of being the "quiet in the land," Mennonite churches in the mid-19th century were just recovering the vision of their forefathers that the Gospel should be shared with all peoples. My own uncle, Paul Wenger, who had endeared himself to us nieces and nephews with his humor and teasing, in 1925 went as a Mennonite missionary to India, a month-long boat trip away.

I was probably most impressed by the gun Uncle Paul bought and tested at our farm before he left. There were wild animals in the part of India he was going to, he said. Sure enough, when he returned for furlough after seven years of work, he brought home a leopard skin, but as I remember it, he had not shot it but had run over it with the mission's Model T Ford! It was, no doubt, a quite romantic vision of missions that sparked my childhood interest.

As I matured I began to entertain the possibility more seriously. I finally came to the place where I could respond to God with Isaiah's words, "Here am I, send me." But I had no clear vision of where I was being sent. "God must want me to serve in some distant, unreached place in the world where the need is greatest," I thought, and joined student prayer groups focusing on Alaska, Tibet and Nepal.

At the same time, unless God made other plans clear, I wanted to serve with the backing of the Mennonite people who had nurtured me in the Christian faith. So I applied to the Board of Missions of our conference. When asked if I sensed God calling me to a specific place in the world, I could only respond that I was interested in those far-away unevangelized peoples.

When the Board of Missions approved me as a candidate, they told me that the place they needed workers most was among the Northern Cheyenne in Montana. Would I be willing?

I had to think about that. The Northern Cheyenne reservation was not much more than a day's drive from my Idaho home. Given our society's view of Indians, this assignment would carry no glamor. I had hardly noticed the Shoshone and Bannock Indian peoples who lived less than 40 miles from my home, although others in my family had. My mother had saved clippings about mission work among those peoples, and an older cousin was teaching in a school that Shoshone and Bannock children attended.

Slowly it dawned on me that I had not outgrown my romantic ideas of missions, that my motives were mixed. Was I concerned about the Gospel or about my own image? Did I want to boast about where I had been? Did I really mean it when I said, "Here am I, send me," or did I just want to bring back a leopard skin?

I offered myself for service among the Northern Cheyenne people. But the Board thought that I had some unfinished business. They did not want to send me there without a partner. Their urging crystallized a conviction that had been growing in my heart and mind for three years, and I invited Esther Boehr to join me in my life and my life's work. We were married December 23, 1943, and by the following March were living among the Northern Cheyenne.

—*Malcolm Wenger*

Esther and Malcolm Wenger.
December 23, 1943—Wisner NE.
(PHOTO BY RABBASS OF WEST POINT, NE)

Our home—Busby MT.

Indians? No. I had never even met
an Indian until Malcolm and I
moved to Busby, Montana, that
March of 1944. I had heard a few
old stories. Bits and pieces. In
1893, when my father was a boy,
his family moved from Henderson
to Wisner, Nebraska. They were met

*Log house with Cheyenne
family.*

at the train by a local Mennonite farmer, and on the way to his home
they passed an Indian camp of several tipis along the Elkhorn River.
Years later, a Winnebago man who was traveling by foot stopped at
my father's farm for a drink. Dad invited him in for food and had a
good visit. In high school I remember hearing that the Indian basket-
ball team from nearby Winnebago was really good, but I never saw
them play.

Missions? Yes. The Penners and the Baumans, Aganetha Fast
and Wilhelmina Kuyf, veteran missionaries from India and China—
all had slept and eaten meals in our home. Missions was table talk in
our home.

My church, Salem Mennonite in Wisner, Nebraska, was a dwin-
dling group of German "Bayerish" immigrants who met in a small,
white-frame building on a plot of land in the same section as my
Dad's farm. Here, too, lay the graves of some of our forefathers.
Although there was no one my age, I felt loved by my church friends,
was taught the Christian faith, and had a desire to share the good
news of Jesus.

In 1940, as a student at Bethel College, I learned to like a rather
mature young man who had already completed three years at The
Bible Institute of Los Angeles. We discovered similar interests as
members of a mission group called Student Volunteers, whose mem-
bers assisted small churches in the area with their services.

After that year we went our separate ways, Malcolm to Illinois to finish college and I to teach rural school in Kansas, but we kept in touch, and in 1943 he asked me if I would join him and go to the Cheyenne. I loved Malcolm and I loved the Lord, but I knew next to nothing about the Cheyenne people and their history! Neither the Petters nor the Habeggers, pioneering missionaries to the Northern Cheyenne, had made it to our Wisner home to tell us about "foreign" missions in our own country. I had much to learn and surely must have seemed a "foreigner" to the Cheyenne people, who were very patient with me.

—*Esther Boehr Wenger*

Busby "Camp" 1950.   *(M. WENGER PHOTO)*

Chapter 1

Traveling From World to World

My face is white.
My heart is brown.

My face is white.
My heart is white.
My joy is tan.

Entering a World of Brown

The world we entered on March 16, 1944, was utterly alien. It was a

world of brown, of braids and buckskin, of hunters and shamans, of feathers, beadwork and dancing. It was a world of unfamiliar rituals around buffalo skulls, of drums beating through the night, of nameless fears and joyous celebrations.

We were the children of hard-working tillers of the soil: planters of seeds, reapers of harvests. Our parents were rooted in German culture, centered in the Mennonite church, thrifty; willing to help their neighbors, yet keeping their distance. They had to be about God's business, seeking to live plain, simple, peace-loving lives.

Blackhawk (Peter Risingsun) asked Malcolm to take his picture.

Malcolm's father farming in Idaho—1920's.

The Northern Cheyenne people in 1944 were a people under pressure. They often felt helpless in the face of irreparable loss. Their hearts had died when the buffalo were slaughtered, when freedom to roam the vast plains was denied, when the elders could no longer guide the destiny of their people.

Their strongest values were under attack. The schools their children were forced to attend taught an alien language and culture. The *Tsemo'ohtavoomase* (Black Robes, Catholics), and the *Ma'eve'ho'e* (Red White Men, Germans, Mennonites) brought new stories about the Creator and new ways of worship. They both built rectangular *ma'heoneeestsemaheonotse* (holy-speaking houses), with rows of benches for their meetings, so different from the circle of the tipi.

Power was in the hands of the white man, whose representative, the *Meave'ho'e* (the reservation superintendent of the Bureau of Indian Affairs), had the final say about many aspects of their lives. He had usurped the powers of the Council of Forty-four Chiefs, many of whom had died in the Indian wars. The men's societies that had once kept order in the tribe had been replaced by Cheyenne police and courts answerable to the white superintendent, not to the people. Nor were these authorities enforcing traditional Cheyenne law but the laws of white society. The *Meave'ho'e* was charged with enacting US government policy: to "civilize, Christianize, and educate the Indian."[3] Indian spiritual leaders were fettered. The government policy-makers seem to have instinctively understood that spiritual practices were the heart of the culture they wished to eradicate. Their methods? Forbid Indian medicine men and women to practice. Outlaw the Sun Dance for 34 years.[4] Drive the worship of the Peyote Eaters underground.

But the first task of the *Meave'ho'e* had been simply to make the Cheyennes stay put on a reservation rather than roaming their former hunting grounds in search of the rapidly disappearing buffalo and other game. A reservation for the Northern Cheyenne had been established in 1884, but there were no longer any buffalo to be found there.[5]

The *Meave'ho'e* had recourse to soldiers to restrain the Cheyennes but the government's main strategy was to issue rations to them every two weeks until the Cheyennes could be taught to farm or to become part of the wage economy. So, to the Cheyenne, the government's man was "the giving white man."

When we arrived on the reservation 60 years after it was established the "Issue House" where rations had been given out still

stood near our home. Though distribution of rations had long since ceased, we heard humorous stories about the first experiences of the Cheyennes with the white man's strange food. The Cheyenne women cooked and cooked the coffee beans they had been issued, but the beans still tasted awful so

"Issue House" at Busby.

they threw them away. Bacon, one man discovered, made quite useful fuel for starting a cooking fire. But what to do with the *penoheo'o*, something white that had been "pounded fine," remained a mystery. The sacks that contained it, though, were obviously valuable, so the Cheyennes dumped out the wheat flour and used the sacks to store and carry things.

In 1936, the government initiated a new experiment in tribal self-government, with an elected council to give Cheyennes some political control. Yet all the council decisions were still subject to the approval of the Secretary of the Interior and the Commissioner of Indian Affairs through their representative, the superintendent. The superintendent still ignored the chiefs, relegating them to ceremonial and religious functions. Since most of the Bureau of Indian Affairs staff did not speak Cheyenne, it was easier for them to deal with younger Cheyenne men who knew a little English. Never mind that these young men lacked status among their people.

Yet this brown world was still the home of rich traditions. The Cheyenne honored courage—courage that did not flinch in the face of death. Cheyenne tradition saw the welfare of all as greater than the achievement of one; valued generosity above accumulation; saw plants and animals as somehow related to people; and honored nature, the source of food and life.

For us fledging missionaries, then, a move of only a few hundred miles from home to share God's good news with others had taken us to a profoundly different world. Here our children were born, grew up, and absorbed much of their outlook on life. What they took in was not quite the way of the Cheyennes nor the way of their parents, but something in-between: a third way. Our children did not choose this world; we chose it for them.

Although we can no longer remember with certainty all the assumptions with which we arrived, we surely expected that we would be teachers. It took many years for us to realize that we would also be learners. Not everything would be white.

Early in our life at Busby we went to a basketball game at the local school. The Cheyenne enjoyed basketball. It was a team sport and they were good at it. Faking a move only to do something else was second nature. They had excellent coordination, smooth team play, no need to be heroes. The players were relaxed, smiling, having fun.

This evening their opponents were boys from a small ranch town miles away. These were the sons of the white ranchers who had replaced the vanished buffalo with white-faced Herefords on rangeland they had been told was "unused."

The Cheyenne team bounded onto the playing floor to the applause of the audience. As the white team followed we were suddenly startled. How wan and pale they looked in the room filled with

beautiful brown faces! That was when it began to sink in. That was
how we, too, appeared to the people among whom we were living. We
were now the odd people, the minority, the different ones.

That was only the beginning of experiencing differences as we
moved back and forth between two peoples, two cultures. The con-
flicts came into sharper focus when we sent our growing children to
the local Bureau of Indian Affairs school as lonely white faces in
brown classes. We were upset when our oldest daughter came home
from school wearing someone else's shoes or sweater. It took us some
time to realize that the Cheyennes had a much more relaxed attitude
toward possessions than we did, and that the children expressed this
by trading clothing.

Teachers, at that time almost exclusively white, tried to encour-
age children to become achievers and to stand out from the group.
"Now, Johnny, you could do as well as Fred if you would just try."
But this was not the Cheyenne way. The individual, they believed,
had to be a part of the group—even subordinate to the group—so all
could survive. "Don't get too smart or we'll take care of you at re-
cess," kids muttered to those too zealous at getting good grades.
Knowledgeable children—our daughter among them—sometimes
feigned ignorance. Acceptance on the playground was too important
to risk standing out.

We suggested to school personnel that local people might be
invited to help bridge the language and cultural gap in the class-
room. They looked at us as if we were from another planet. We
wondered if the teaching process could build on the Cheyenne sense
of community, with the more skilled helping the group advance to-
gether rather than singling out individual achievers. These ideas
were too foreign. Our suggestions became mired in the molasses of
government bureaucracy, never to be tried until years later.

World War II and its aftermath disrupted schools on the North-
ern Cheyenne reservation. Teachers were suddenly scarce. When

our daughter Ann entered first grade in 1954 her teacher was trained to teach high school, and just moved too fast for six-year-olds. Not until third grade did an experienced teacher take the class back to the primers and help them learn to read. One year Ann's "classroom" was the stage of the auditorium. At times the class got out of control.

We noticed Ann's growing reluctance to go to school. There were times when she was the only white child in her classroom and became the target of Cheyenne frustration. It was difficult and costly to live in two cultures and try to satisfy the expectations of both.

We were also fearful that our children might adopt values different from our own as they learned to see life through the eyes of their playmates. We had not yet realized that some things the Cheyenne valued, such as generosity, might prove to be closer to the teachings of Jesus than, for example, our legendary Mennonite thrift.

We wondered what to do. Home schooling, which might have eased some of the stress, somehow did not enter our minds. It just wasn't done in those days. Our energies were fully occupied in learning the Cheyenne language and carrying on our work in the church and community. We finally decided that our daughters might be better off with at least some experience in one of "our" (white) communities. Friends offered to take in Ann so that she could attend seventh grade in a one-room rural school near Freeman, South Dakota. Her older sister stayed with grandparents in Mountain Lake, Minnesota, and the next year our whole family spent the winter there. I remember some twinges of guilt as we sent our daughters away to school. Were we abandoning a school on the reservation that we should be helping to improve? We had options that our Cheyenne friends did not have.

What we didn't anticipate was that even in these "better" schools conflict would remain. Ann somehow felt that she was really Indian and in some ways alien in the all-white school.

More than anyone else in the family, Ann absorbed Cheyenne ways of thinking and feeling. To be sure, this was mixed with a good dose of parental culture. Stubbornly rooted in our own ways of thinking and doing, we only slowly understood that she fit into a unique niche somewhere between our values and those of the Cheyenne people. We didn't quite get "tanned," as she did, just a little less pale.

Ann's school in South Dakota.

(PHOTO COURTESY ANN WENGER—GOSHEN, IN)

Chapter 2

This Brown Laughter

They say you used to sleep
with a gun under your pillow.
I don't know about that.

Did you know that you left
a trail of sunshine inside of me?
Your love came down to me.

You weren't laughing
when I turned up grown with new ideas.
Can the difference take yesterday away?

I remember being young,
loving you for teasing me,
knowing that you laughed right into my soul.

When Death reached for me, sixteen,
that day in Tongue River's waters,
you pushed him away.

Someday I'll dance for this joy
and set my crown on your head

for giving me a place
to laugh.

17

The Missing Bridge and the Useless Gun

I slammed on the brakes of our '36 Chevy sedan. Where the bridge over Stebbins Creek should have been was an empty gap. No barrier, just space. We were on a winding trail through the hills between Lame Deer and Ashland, Montana, that in those days saw only an occasional car. A bulldozer, it seems, had crashed through the old wooden bridge the day before. The dozer had been able to pull itself out of the wreckage and continue down the road but there was no way our old car could follow in its tracks.

Barely six months had passed since we had joined the Mennonite mission staff on the Northern Cheyenne reservation. We were immersed in an entirely new way of life about which we still knew very little. We were bursting with questions, but were just beginning to develop close friendships with Cheyenne people and were unsure how inquisitive we should be.

Our co-workers with their years of experience could have helped us, but we discovered that staff meetings were held only once a year, and then only if the mission chairman felt it was necessary. Rodolphe Petter was a veteran of the days when most local travel was by horse-drawn vehicle, and missionaries in the field had to "go it alone." Having lived with the Cheyenne for many years, and speaking their language fluently, he did not feel the need for the more frequent fellowship and discussion we craved.

Then, too, it was wartime. Gas and tires were rationed. The national speed limit was 35 miles per hour. The Japanese attack on Pearl Harbor had aborted the building of a new road across the reservation. The grade was finished between Crow Agency and Lame Deer, but no gravel or crushed rock had been put on it, and heavy rain could immobilize a car in sticky gumbo and force its occupants to walk out. Through the forested hills between Lame Deer and

Ashland, we had the choice of two trails, neither of which looked ready for two-way traffic. A decision to drive somewhere was not taken lightly.

When Esther's mother and father came by train for a two-week visit we saw it as an opportunity to show them the other communities on the reservation and visit our co-workers. We could also try out our "new" car. Actually, no new cars were being made for civilians at that time. We were fortunate to find an eight-year-old sedan that a rural mail carrier had given up on.

Leaving Busby, we picked up Mrs. Rodolphe Petter at Lame Deer and took the Stebbins Creek road on to Ashland to visit with Laura Petter, her widowed daughter-in-law, whom we barely knew. With only seven miles left of our 40-mile journey, we faced the broken bridge. What should we do? We could go back to Lame Deer and then take the trail up Soldier Gulch and down Logging Creek, but that would probably take two additional hours.

Young and brash, I asked the others to get out of the car, picked a spot a bit upstream and gunned the car through the cattails. The creek was little more than a car's length across but in spite of the car's speed it sank decisively into the mud as if it planned to spend the rest of its career there.

While my passengers picked wild plums and enjoyed a picnic lunch on a grassy spot in the green, tree-dotted hills, I started the long hot walk into Ashland. I had plenty of time to think about my foolishness. Cattails meant soft mud. That was no place to try to ford a creek. I did meet a Cheyenne man with a team and wagon and told him of my predicament. Fortunately he understood some English. He did not laugh but wisely declined to try to pull the car out with the team. It would not have budged.

Arriving at the Ashland parsonage I told my story. Laura Petter assured me that her co-worker, *Homa'ehesta* (Beaver Heart), whom she introduced by his English name, Ike Shoulderblade, would help out this embarrassed missionary. Beaver Heart drove Laura's car out to pick up my stranded passengers and gently pointed out a place a couple hundred feet downstream where one could easily ford the creek on the gravelly bottom. He took us to Lame Deer for the night. The next day a truck from the Indian Agency road department deliv-

Beaver Heart (Ike Shoulderblade)

ered a culvert to replace the bridge and pulled our car out of the mud. We were even able to go on to Ashland, have dinner with Laura Petter, and drive to Birney for a visit before returning to Busby. That was when I really began to appreciate Beaver Heart.

After some months the mission staff responded to our need for more frequent meetings. Those gatherings became much more than business meetings. We ate together, laughed together and cried together. There was teasing and storytelling. Laura Petter's natural children Valdo and Amy, and her adopted children Darlene and Amelia, were still at home, as were children to whom she was giving foster care. So these gatherings took on some of the feel of a family reunion.

Beaver Heart paid special attention to the children. "There's Annie, Annie get your gun," he would say when he saw Ann, repeating a phrase picked up, perhaps, from the radio. Blood relatives lived miles away and we saw them no more than once a year, so these people became family away from family.

Sometimes Ike's brother, *Nahkoheo'emoxo'eha* (Bear Sole), whom we usually called James Shoulderblade, and his wife *Ma'heonehoehne'e* (Medicine Coming Out Woman), Julia, would join us at these meetings. Bear Sole and Medicine Coming Out Woman were leaders in the Petter Memorial Mennonite Church in Lame Deer and also helped with the church work in Birney.

We looked forward to the home prayer meetings that they often arranged. They once told us that they had had gatherings in more than 100 homes in Lame Deer alone. Often, non-Christians who were facing difficulty would invite the Christians over to pray for them. Much of the conversation would be in Cheyenne and Bear Sole would lead us in singing indigenous gospel songs. Unlike the church's book of hymns that had been translated from English and German into Cheyenne, these songs, composed mostly by Cheyenne Christians in Oklahoma, used Indian musical forms.

These Cheyenne melodies, at first unfamiliar, gradually became enjoyable. David Graber, the musician who later transcribed many of these songs in the hymn book, *Cheyenne Spiritual Songs*, told us that Cheyenne music used four, five, or six-tone scales rather than the eight-tone scale with which we were familiar. The texts usually focused on a single truth of the Christian faith.

Often, at the end of a prayer meeting, the hostess would serve a lunch and then there was time for stories and jokes. Bear Sole told us that his father once walked more than 1,000 miles from Montana to "Indian Territory" (Oklahoma) to visit relatives, living off the country as he went. We laughed at the story of *Totseske'matsenehe* (Tiny Eyes), who had so often found the gate to his haystack open and his hay being eaten up by cattle, that he resolved to take care of it once and for all. With barbed wire and staples he nailed the gate solidly shut. "There, no one's going to open that gate again," he said. Only then did he realize that he and his team and wagon were on the wrong side of the fence. Such a person, James assured us, was automatically a member of the "Turtle Clan," the Cheyenne equivalent of the "absent-minded professor."

Before his marriage, Bear Sole had fought in Europe in the Second World War. A young Cheyenne woman, Medicine Coming Out Woman, encouraged Cheyenne Christians to write to the men in the Army. She herself wrote to Bear Sole and when he returned after the war, she married him. This caused much concern among the Christians because Bear Sole was not a Christian and had already fathered a child.

Many things happened during the war, and especially in battle, that Bear Sole was reluctant to talk about. He had seen men break down and cry like babies in the midst of the killing. That he had never done: Cheyenne men don't cry. Bear Sole came back from Europe with a chip on his shoulder. No one, he had decided, no one, especially not a white man, would ever push him around again. To make sure of that, he always carried a concealed handgun.

But the Christians befriended Bear Sole and kept praying for him. Once he stayed overnight with his brother at Laura Petter's place. The next morning Laura was making the bed that the guest had occupied. As fluffed up the pillow, she discovered the gun he had hidden there and forgotten. Startled, she thought for a moment and then replaced the pillow over the gun, finished making the bed and left the room.

Occasionally Bear Sole came to church. One night we gathered at Lame Deer to hear a talk by a visiting missionary to the Hopi Indians, John Suderman, from Oraibi, Arizona. The old log church was full and Bear Sole was there with his wife. The visiting preacher closed the service with an invitation for anyone who wanted to make a decision to follow Christ to come forward. No one responded.

People began to leave. Then someone noticed that James was sitting alone, crying. The Christians gathered around him, and he decided to start down the Jesus trail. As he later described it, he felt as though his feet were not even touching the floor as he walked out of church. We heard no more about the gun.

Chapter 3

Brown Castration

You are a stallion
strong, wild, courageous, gorgeous,
Yet clutching the dying
in your dark brown soul.
You are fast, sleek, tough, intelligent,
but hate smears the colors in your gut.
You are poured forth in the sun,
watered in the moon,
polished by the grasses.

Pull out the knife of castration
driven by white greed.
Rise and be brown.

▃ Stands in Timber and the Buffalo

The guard at the door of the Manitoba legislative building told us that he was just about to lock up for the day. We explained that we were visitors from the United States attending the triennial Mennonite conference nearby and had hoped to see the huge bronze buffalo, symbol of the province of Manitoba, that we had heard was inside the building.

The guard look quizzically at *Ma'taa'ohnee'setse* (Stands in Timber), whom we had introduced as a delegate to the conference. We could almost hear his unspoken question, "What is this Indian guy doing at a Mennonite conference?" Most Manitobans knew about Mennonites, but Indian Mennonites? His curiosity piqued, the guard decided to bend the rules and let us in for a brief look. Soon we were standing by the buffalo and Stands in Timber was enlightening the guard on the fine points of hunting, skinning, and butchering buffalo. The guard no doubt had an interesting excuse for getting home late that night.

John Stands in Timber.

I, too, was impressed with Stands in Timber's knowledge of the buffalo hunt. He had been only two years old in 1884 when President Chester A. Arthur ordered a tiny part of the former hunting grounds of the Northern Cheyenne "reserved" for them to live on. That was the year the last wild buffalo was killed on what is now the Northern Cheyenne Indian Reservation. Yet here was Stands in Timber, a man educated in the white man's boarding schools away from the reservation, with intimate knowledge of buffalo hunting. He had listened well to his elders.

For many years the buffalo had been the source of life for the Cheyenne and other Plains Indians. Buffalo hides covered their movable homes and formed the soles of their shoes. Buffalo robes protected them from the bitter cold of the northern winters. They ate more buffalo meat than anything else. They sewed their clothing with sinew from the buffalo's back. They crafted buffalo bones into tools. They measured a man's worth—at least in part—by his skill in hunting the buffalo. Inside the *Hoxeheome*, the "lodge of purification" in which the last part of the great Cheyenne ceremonial of cleansing and renewal known as the Sun Dance takes place, is an altar built around the skull of a buffalo.

Thirty million buffalo once ranged this land from the mountains of Pennsylvania to the delta of the Mississippi and from Northern Mexico to Great Slave Lake, says historian E. Douglas Branch. In an epic slaughter during the 1870s and the 1880s "the western herd of over seven million buffaloes was shattered and annihilated, and barely eighty scarred fugitives were left."[6] Indians saw this compulsive killing, in which most of the buffalo carcasses were left to rot, as a kind of white man's insanity.

In 1886 the directors of the National Museum in Washington, DC, realized that the buffalo were nearly gone and that they had no presentable specimens for an exhibit. It took most of a year to locate a lonely herd of 35 buffalo in the badlands north of the Yellowstone River in Montana. In a hunt that lasted from mid-October to December, the museum obtained 20 skins. Nearly every full-grown bull that was killed carried several old bullets in its body. Taxidermist William Hornaday's report to the Smithsonian was "the first careful history of the butchery that had dirtied the West, and became the textbook of those men who succeeded, ultimately, in making the American government understand its obligation [to protect the surviving buffalo]."[7]

For almost 20 years during and after this huge slaughter, buffalo bones were big business. Freight trains headed East loaded with bones destined for fertilizer and for carbon for sugar refineries. In 1874 alone, the Santa Fe Railroad shipped seven million tons of bones. This vast harvest remained despite the loss of millions of pounds to prairie fires.[8]

"It is only thirty years ago [about 1899]," writes historian E. Douglas Branch, "that a band of Indians, in the spring, saddled their ponies and rode away—as of old, but in silence and sadness."

> "Where are you bound?" some white man asks and they
>   answer,
> "For the buffalo."
> "But there are no more."
> "No, we know it."
> "Then why are you going on such a foolish chase?"
> "Oh, we always go at this time; maybe we shall find some."[9]

Loss of the buffalo and restriction to the reservation was devastating to the Cheyenne man who defined himself by skill in the hunt and bravery in warfare. How could he prove his manhood when all war parties had ceased? And where would a young man get the horses to give his bride's family if not from raiding another tribe? How could he win a desirable bride if he could not prove his bravery? A man was not yet a man until he had demonstrated bravery in the face of the enemy. Only then was he celebrated by the whole tribe, ceremonially given a new name, and considered "grown up." I began to understand why defeated Cheyenne warriors almost immediately joined the white man's army as scouts, and why military service continues to attract Cheyenne youth today.

So what does a hunter do when the game is all gone? The government's answer: he becomes a farmer. Initially government officials hoped that this transition could be accomplished rather quickly. But it did not take long to discover that small farming on buffalo range was a precarious and unreliable venture. With a short growing season, drought, hail, plagues of grasshoppers, forest and grass fires, and the failure of irrigation schemes, the Cheyennes had little choice but to depend on government rations.[10] Although at one time enough wheat was raised on the reservation to support a flour mill in Lame Deer, on the whole, the hunter could no longer feed his family.

Cattle raising, a closer fit with old Cheyenne ways, initially showed promise. But in 1914 the government decided to force Indian cattle owners, under threat of jail time, to put their cattle in a government-controlled tribal herd. The tribal herd was a disaster: Within 12 years, two-thirds of Cheyenne-owned cattle perished. According to a study by a Senate committee released in 1930, this loss amounted to some one million dollars.[11] When we arrived in Montana in the 1940s our nearest neighbor was the "government farmer" who was still trying to help turn Cheyennes into farmers.

Other government aid programs wrought unanticipated changes in Cheyenne society. "Aid to Dependent Children" checks went to the woman. Having a man in the home was sometimes more of a liability than a help in putting food on the table. "Aid to the Aged" turned upside down the Cheyenne tradition that those able to hunt shared first with those who could not. Now younger people began living off of income intended to help the elderly.

Wage-earning jobs were few, but Cheyennes showed that they could do well in them. Once the Indian Bureau's forestry department hired Cheyennes to thin so-called "dog hair growth"—that multitude of small pine trees that sprouted in rare wet years but could not thrive in the dry years that followed. We noticed that men with jobs stood taller, drank less alcohol, and stayed out of jail.

Our missionary predecessor, Alfred Habegger, was one of the few whites that spoke Cheyenne. He also had one of the few tel-

ephones in Busby in the early days. Many Cheyennes had to undergo
the humiliation of conducting much of their business with the au-
thorities—getting permission to slaughter a cow for food, or inquir-
ing about lease income from land they owned—on the missionary's
phone and through his interpretation.

Sadly, the Christian church was nearly as slow as the govern-
ment in turning responsibility over to Cheyenne leaders. We failed to
follow the Mennonite tradition of congregations choosing their own
self-supporting leaders. Instead we missionaries modeled a pattern
of dependence on the support of the wider church, on the paycheck
from church "headquarters."

As I gradually learned Cheyenne history it was no longer such a
puzzle to me why so many Cheyenne men (and later women) turned
to alcohol, became depressed, and even committed suicide. Today,
with more jobs available, with better housing built by the Northern
Cheyenne Housing Authority, many Cheyennes are doing well, hold-
ing responsible jobs and supporting their families. Yet, population
growth is racing ahead of the available jobs.

A few years ago when we returned to Montana to attend Cheyenne
Christian Family Camp in the beautiful forested hills east of Lame
Deer, our former neighbor, Jason Whiteman, took us in his pickup
truck to find the buffalo herd now owned by the Cheyenne people.
They initially had tried to get a start from the herd in Yellowstone
National Park, but found the requirements and paperwork daunting.
Finally, Lutheran rancher T. R. Hughes, who raised buffalo in Ne-
braska, provided a small herd to give them a start.

After driving for nearly an hour we finally spotted part of the
100-head tribal herd. Already the Cheyennes were beginning to eat
buffalo meat again on special occasions. Jason was environmental
officer and buffalo wrangler for the tribe. He told us that keeping the
bulls fenced in was almost impossible but that the cows usually
stayed in the range the Cheyenne had fenced off for them.

As we talked to one of the old men at the camp we saw the joy in his face as he said, "Buffalo calves are being born on Cheyenne land again." And as we work with Cheyenne brothers and sisters on the Mennonite Indian Leaders Council we sense some of the old pride and wisdom being freed to serve Cheyenne people again. The knife has been pulled out and the wound has begun to heal.

Buffalo from the Cheyenne herd.

Chapter 4

A Child's Vision in Brown

I pass intimidated
through these sand hills
behind my house.
They say the spirits rest here
and holy men use this place.
I, too, feel that they do.
I have seen offerings—
cloth and five stones.

I pass in the dusk,
heart huddled in fear.
Small friends whisper
of yesterday's dead.
The casket is gone but
in the shadowed church
the spirits are alive.
Best to circle around.

His long braids falling
to his shoulder
tell me he is a holy man.
I stay at a distance.

He will eat peyote tonight
and see visions, maybe.
I will hear his drums
before I sleep

I hear a coyote howl.
I don't like that sound.
I think he stands on the hill
where the sun rests before leaving.

The sound of drums
brings monotonous comfort.

"Prayer cloth" near Busby cemetery.

(PHOTO BY M. WENGER—1948)

Spirits, Tornado and Peyote

As a child I had learned little about spirits. I was, of course, familiar
with the stories of Jesus freeing people from dangerous and destruc-
tive demons. I knew from the book of Hebrews that Christian hospi-
tality might involve hosting angels without being aware of it. But
unseen spirits were not a part of my life in a way that would have
struck fear or brought unexpected joy.

I do remember one old story about the death of a neighbor in
which a witness, at the moment of death, saw a dark sphere roll out
from under the bed, across the floor, and vanish. I could tell from the
reaction of the adults about me that this was not considered a normal
way for a person's spirit to leave the body.

But in this new brown world in which we were yet strangers,
another reality prevailed. Unseen spirits were real and powerful and
had to be reckoned with daily. Our children learned more about this
from their playmates than we did. After death the Cheyenne believed
the *seoto* (souls) of the departed lingered for four days before finding
"the trail where the footprints all pointed the same way."

This trail took the *seoto* to the bright star path in the sky which
led to *seano* (the camp of the dead). It was best to deal with the body
of a person who had died as soon as possible and be careful during
those four days because the *seo'otse*, the ghost of the dead person,
might want to take someone, especially a child, along for company
on the trail.[12]

Over the years, I was to learn again and again how powerfully
close the spirit world was to our own in Cheyenne minds. One Sun-
day evening at Busby, as I was walking with a group of boarding
school students through the darkness across the field to the church, I
noticed that one young boy seemed white-faced and withdrawn. I
asked what was troubling him. He said that he had walked into the
bathroom at the school dormitories a short while before and there,

lying on the floor, was the body of his mother—the mother who had frozen to death a week before while in a drunken stupor.

In Oklahoma a Cheyenne woman was telling me about her husband who had died a few days earlier while in a motel room with another woman. "Two nights ago," she said, "my teenage daughters were walking to town and someone called out to them. It was the voice of their father." She herself had heard his footsteps as he crossed the bedroom floor in the darkness. Cheyennes used cedar branches to protect themselves from the spirits of the dead but even this was not working for her. We prayed for God's presence and protection.

On a bitterly cold winter night in Lame Deer, I was meeting with the church council of the Mennonite church. We decided to move the meeting to the office of the tribal housing authority, which was already warm, rather than trying to heat up the frigid church. Later that evening, business over, we sat telling stories.

Council Member Virginia Toews, then director of the tribal housing program, pointed to the receptionist's desk where a printing calculator stood. "We had been having difficulty with that calculator," she said. "It would suddenly start printing numbers when no one was using it. We thought there must be some short circuit in it and sent it in to Billings for repairs. The repairman could find nothing wrong with it. But when we brought it back to the office, it would again unexpectedly start printing numbers on its own—usually high numbers. This was especially disconcerting when I was working alone late at night."

"I told the story of the calculator to some of my Cheyenne friends," Virginia went on, "and they said that they could help out. They brought in a branch of a cedar tree and told me to lay it on top of the file near the calculator. I did, and we haven't had any trouble since."

One summer we had visitors from Alberta, Curley Rider and his wife and another companion (all Blood Indians) and two Mennonite lay missionaries. Walks On the Ground, a Cheyenne elder and new

Christian, wanted to tell a story to the guests. Because his English was limited and he did not speak the language of the Blood people, he asked if I would interpret from Cheyenne to English.

Busby chapel before the tornado.

He told of a time years before when Mennonite missionaries had lived just a few years among the Northern Cheyenne and had built a log chapel at Busby. A Cheyenne *ma'heonehetane* (medicine man), a man of power who was feared for his ability to control whirlwinds, was disturbed by the work of the missionaries and decided to put a stop to it. He placed a curse on the log chapel. Later a tornado, a very rare occurrence in that area, tore through the churchyard and flattened the chapel. Pieces of the building were found 10 miles away on Muddy creek. The nearby parsonage and log house were hardly touched.

This seemed to me an odd story to share with visiting Christians from another tribe. Why tell about a man who had learned to manipulate spirit power for his own ends? Would it not have been better

Busby chapel after 1914 tornado.

to tell something that more clearly demonstrated the power of God over the unseen forces of evil?

Walks On the Ground had no doubt that the power of the shaman was responsible for what had happened. But he wasn't finished. "There were three things," he said, "that survived the storm unharmed." One was the "place where the word of God is preached" (the pulpit). The others were the stove and the reed organ.

"This man," he said, "was trying to stop the preaching of the gospel,

Esther tells the story of the reed organ—1986.

but he failed. It is still being preached from the very same pulpit. He tried to destroy our joy as Christians, but we still sing from the same books [protected when the pulpit fell over them], to the music of the same organ. Even our fellowship [symbolized by the warmth of the stove] is still strong. He failed. He is now dead and his power is dead with him."

Later as I looked at an old picture of the ruined church, I wondered why God had allowed things to turn out that way. Perhaps it had as much to do with deepening my understanding of the realities of the unseen world as it did with showing God's ways to the Cheyenne or Blood people. As the apostle Paul reminded us, "For our struggle is not against flesh and blood, but against...the spiritual forces of evil in the heavenly realms" (Ephesians 6:12). No wonder Cheyennes had palpable fear of unseen powers. Biblical language that spoke of the Christian life as a spiritual battle became more meaningful to me.

Is it possible, I wondered, that the enemy uses different tactics in a society like mine where science has cast deep doubts on the

Walks On The Ground telling a story.

existence of a spiritual realm? Perhaps here was a people that could understand better than I what Jesus was about when he instructed his disciples to cast out demons. Or when he said, "In this world you will have trouble. But take heart! I have overcome the world" (John 16:33).

There was a more recent spiritual tradition among the Cheyenne that deliberately invoked the spirit world through the use of peyote. Awakened from sleep late at night in the mission parsonage I often heard the distant monotonous throb of the peyote drum. I could visualize the canvas tipi that stood near a log cabin somewhere in Busby village. Flickering flames of a ceremonial fire would cast the shadows of a group of men engaged in all-night worship. One would shake a gourd rattle, another would beat a water drum (a cast iron kettle with some water and charcoal inside and a skin tied over its open mouth); all would take turns singing special peyote songs. Peyote "buttons," the dried top of a carrot-shaped cactus that grows wild in Texas and Mexico, would be eaten or drunk as "tea." This would induce visions and open the door to another reality.

Peyote Tipi in Busby.

The Southern Cheyennes had learned the peyote "road" from the Kiowa and Comanche. Leonard Tyler, a Southern Cheyenne, then brought the knowledge of peyote to the Northern Cheyennes. Coincidentally, this happened at about the same time that Rodolphe Petter, Mennonite missionary to the

Southern Cheyenne, made his first visits to the Northern Cheyennes in 1898. Oddly enough, Petter and Tyler actually knew each other.

Some Cheyenne *Mataheve'hanaheo'o* (Peyote Eaters), as they called themselves, saw their worship as an Indian version of Christianity. They used Christian symbols and the Bible in their services. They sang, confessed their sins, saw other-worldly visions, and enjoyed fellowship with each other.

Peyote was also used as a medicine for illness. *Konape* (John Woodenlegs), former tribal chairman and leader of the Peyote Eaters, told of a dying woman who was carried into the peyote tipi to be treated. The participants feared she would die during the service. In the morning, though, she was able to walk out with the others.[13]

While some Cheyennes attended both peyote worship and Christian church services, the missionaries who had been my mentors were unanimous in their opposition to peyote. "Peyote," they said, "has taken the place of Christ as the way to God and is therefore idolatrous." They supported the government's efforts to outlaw peyote use. Declaring peyote illegal, however, only forced peyote eaters to worship in secret. One creek where they met on the Northern Cheyenne reservation is known as Peyote Creek to this day.

As I lay awake listening to the drums in the 1940s, peyote was no longer illegal. Government policy had changed in the 1930s and no longer prohibited Indian religions, to the dismay of those who had supported the ban. The Peyote Eaters had formally organized as the Native American Church and stated that they used peyote as a sacrament as Christians use bread and wine.[14]

The peyote church appealed to the Cheyennes. It used Indian forms in worship, and Indian people felt at home there. John Woodenlegs described the use of peyote as "the native way of worship" in contrast to Christianity which he saw as "the white man's way of worship."[15] The use of peyote has continued to spread to new tribal groups in the United States and Canada.

The privilege of some long talks with Harold Turner, a Christian scholar noted for his studies of African Independent Churches, gave me some new insights about the success and spread of the peyote "road." Many indigenous African churches developed because the gospel had come in a foreign dress, and Africans wanted to express their faith in African forms. Was the Native American Church a similar protest against the "white man's way of worship?" Looking back, I wonder if it was wise to support the use of coercive government power in banning peyote.

The discovery that Christianity was for all people—not just the white man—helped some Cheyennes to become Christians. Clearly, though, we white missionaries had hindered this understanding by offering Cheyennes the "living water" in a white man's cup.

Chapter 5

Country Store

The opening door sounded the bell
entering another world:
the smell of new tires,
foot-carved wooden floors,
candy perched in boxes behind the glass,
little boxed holes with mail sticking out.

Out in the middle of the valley,
hay fields and white-faced cattle,
This place was so special.
Was it the shining knotty pine wall?
the rag rugs,
the rocking chairs in this house to the back?
the tiny gray-haired lady?

Somehow the light was brighter
those Sunday afternoons,
the creek valley lighter,
the sky more brilliant,
the bubbling water clearer.

When you all get up there
ask for a little gray-haired lady
from Kirby store.

She probably doesn't know it,
but she has my star in her crown.

▄ Of Mixed Bloods and Battles

With my hand on the saddle horn and my foot in the stirrup I started to mount the pony. The next moment I was lying flat in the dust of the corral. This spirited steed was nothing like the gentle work horses of my youth. Then too, hurrying to saddle the horse I had clumsily caught the opposite stirrup under the cinch. When my weight drove the stirrup into the horse's side, he quite properly bucked me off.

It was an inauspicious start to the first Sunday that our co-workers were away from Busby. I was responsible for not only the morning service and the evening service with perhaps 50 children from the government boarding school, but also for an afternoon Sunday School at Kirby on the Upper Rosebud. Not yet owning a car, I had saddled up to ride 10 miles or so to the makeshift building, once a frame for a tent, now enclosed and roofed with tarpaper, where the Sunday School met.

I picked myself up, caught the horse, refastened the cinch and started out. For about a mile I rode along the "highway," nicely graded but unsurfaced. When a noisy car approached in a cloud of

Summer Bible School at Kirby.

dust I thought for a moment that my already jittery mount either was going to jump off the high bank of the road into a marshy area along Rosebud creek or buck me off again. Somehow I got him quieted again and went on. Five or six miles into the ride it became clear that the horse would never make it. He just hadn't been ridden enough yet that spring. I decided to turn back.

On other Sunday afternoons I did make it to Kirby, not far from the southern boundary of the Northern Cheyenne Reservation. The boundary was marked only by a cattle guard, a grid of pipes or rails across a depression in the road that discouraged cattle and horses from crossing but allowed vehicles across. Cattle guards are common in range country, but this one divided more than cattle. It divided the Northern Cheyennes and the whites, two deeply different and mutually distrustful cultures.

Or perhaps it was really three cultures. Some "Cheyennes" could name ancestors from many other tribes—Pawnee, Crow, Sioux, Arapaho, and Assiniboine. Some from both sides simply ignored the barriers between Indian and white, married and raised children, children of a third culture. People often called them "half-breeds" or just "breeds" but usually not to their face. Jim Wilson was one of these. A British sailor, some said he was, who somehow ended up on the Northern Cheyenne Reservation and married Martha Yellow Eagle. We got the impression that neither of them really learned to speak the other's language, but they appeared devoted to each other and raised at least 10 bilingual children.

I no longer remember how a Swedish family, the Lithanders, came to rent land on the reservation. As we entered their neat log cabin for the first time we were startled to see a bookshelf covering an entire wall. Coming from Europe, they found it strange that government schools did not provide religious instruction for children, and decided to allow us to pick up their son Lars for Kirby Sunday School. So a Lithander joined the Bad Horses, Smalls, Bixbys, Fighting Bears, Roundstones, Grasshoppers, Killsontops, and other full-blood or mixed-blood people who attended or sent their children.

Not far upstream from the Kirby cattle guard, Rosebud valley narrowed and permitted only cramped hay fields to the white ranchers who ran their cattle on the hills on either side. A few dark green ponderosa pines graced the steep slopes. A strip of red shale cut through the green grass of spring where the hills had been gouged to make a road up the side of the valley. Here, shaded by cottonwoods, lay the Kirby Store.

The store offered a little of most of the things ranchers needed: a post office, groceries, barbed wire, nails. The closest supermarket was 50 miles farther down the curving red shale road. I wondered whether the store made enough profit to live on, but the Furmans who operated it seemed content.

One problem with the little outpost Sunday School was that we had no way to heat the shelter in which we met. When we learned that a small Sunday School for area ranchers was meeting at Kirby store, we explored the possibility of meeting together. They welcomed us. So those of us who had been meeting on the reservation joined the Furmans, the Pensons, the Taylors, and others—people of

Malcolm with class at Kirby Store.

three cultures meeting, a bit hesi-
tantly at first, around the word of
God.

To one who knew the not-too-
distant history of these peoples,
there were plenty of reasons why
such a peaceful gathering was im-
probable at best. I hold in my hand
an ancient buffalo tooth, excavated
by a rancher from an old "buffalo

Tooth from "buffalo jump."
(R. VOTH PHOTO)

jump" on his land, a few miles upstream from Kirby store. The tooth
dates back before "the time of the horse" when the old ones hunted
by stampeding buffalo over a cut bank. The tooth reminds me how
close we whites came to killing all the buffalo, the very source of life
to the Cheyennes.

Not far from this buffalo jump and only some 75 years earlier, on
the morning of June 16, 1876, a column of about a thousand soldiers
accompanied by Crow and Shoshoni scouts under the command of
General George F. Crook stopped for coffee. They were part of a
large military campaign to force the Sioux and Cheyennes out of the
"unceded territory" west of the Black Hills and onto reservations.
This, in turn, would open up vast areas of grassland to white cattle-
men.

Catching the mobile Indians had always been the army's prob-
lem. But on this day, Sioux and Cheyenne warriors surprised Crook's
men, and unexpectedly pressed their attack for six hours of some of
the fiercest fighting of the Indian wars before they withdrew. Both
sides suffered losses, though just how many is a matter of contro-
versy. One account lists 64 killed and 119 wounded from both sides.[16]
General Crook retreated south to Goose Creek (now Sheridan, Wyo-
ming) to await reinforcements. The Indians returned to their camps
on the Little Big Horn River, about 25 miles to the northwest.

Ten days later another military column led by Yellow Hair (George Armstrong Custer), met disaster when it attacked that camp. A stunned Congress voted to add 2,500 more cavalrymen to the army and build two new forts on the Yellowstone.[17] The search for Indian villages continued through the following winter. When the army discovered one, it attacked, destroying food and shelter, and killing or capturing horses.

Ultimately the Sioux and the Cheyenne surrendered. There were just too many soldiers, too many white people. Many of the Northern Cheyenne were pressured to go to Indian Territory (now Oklahoma), the catchall location for tribes deprived of their homes, fields and hunting grounds. Although their relatives the Southern Cheyenne already had a reservation there, the northerners were homesick. Many of their children and old people died of malaria and measles. They asked for permission to return to the north. The government refused, but about 300 left anyway, led by *Vooheheeve* (Morning Star), also known as Dull Knife, and *O'komoxhaahketa* (Little Coyote), known in English as Little Wolf.

It proved to be an epic trip north. Harassed continuously by a massive army hunt, they eventually separated, Morning Star's group heading toward the Sioux at Red Cloud's Agency, while Little Wolf's

Mrs. Pine, Cheyenne elder.

wintered in the Sand Hills. But Red Cloud Agency had been moved, and in a snowstorm Morning Star's group ran right into soldiers from Fort Robinson. Taken to the Fort, they were at first treated well, but then orders came from Washington that they must go back to Indian Territory.

When they refused, saying they would rather die, they were imprisoned in a barracks without food, water or fuel. On a bitterly cold January night they made a desperate attempt to break out. About 60, half of the group, were killed. Under public pressure the army relented and permitted them to join the Sioux at Red Cloud Agency.

Finally the Northern Cheyenne were allowed to choose land for a reservation. They picked an area between Tongue River and Rosebud Creek for its plentiful water, wood and grass. That area, later enlarged to receive the Cheyennes from Red Cloud Agency, became the Northern Cheyenne reservation.[18]

Many years later I stood with a Cheyenne friend, *Aenohe Oxhaa'eho'ostse* (High Hawk) better known to us as Ted Risingsun, looking at the site of the desperate dash for freedom from Fort Robinson. High Hawk told me that there was no known burial site for his relatives and others who died there. One hundred and eighteen years after the event the Smithsonian Institution and Harvard University's Peabody Museum returned the remains of 26 Cheyenne men, women and children that had been given to them by the army for "scientific study." *Mahpevena'hane* (Kills on Water), Leonard Little Wolf, was there when the Cheyennes buried the bones of these relatives at Busby where survivors of Morning Star's band had settled. With tears in his eyes, he told us that the most heartbreaking sight was the skull of small girl with a bullet hole through the forehead. She had been between three and five years old.

This was not ancient history. These things had happened to the parents and grandparents of the people we lived with. That some of them could meet together with whites and treat them as brothers and sisters was a special gift. For a time one of those meeting places was Kirby Store.

Decades later we drove by Kirby on a new black-topped road. The hills and the stream had not visibly changed, but the store was gone, gutted by a fire. Today people of the three cultures still meet at Kirby, attracted by a different spirit: Kirby store has been replaced by a bar.

Chapter 6

An Uncle in Brown

When I was still a pigtail-swinging little girl,
making blanket tents out on the fence,
and playing with baby dolls,
That's when I knew you.

And you taught me my Sunday School,
and I just knew that you could fly
and catch the yellow moon.

When I gave up baby dolls and mud pies,
for playing hide-and-seek by night,
that's when you told your wife good-bye.

You took your shiny lady and your booze.
You took my believing,
because I just knew that you could fly
and catch the yellow moon that touched the hill.

Yesterday they told me you were dead.
Died an alcoholic, they said.
I cried, because I just knew...

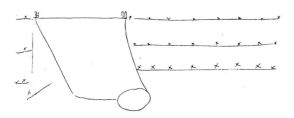

Twenty Stands and Walks On the Ground

There are strange things about prayer. Jesus assures us that we need not worry because the heavenly father knows what we need before we ask. Yet he insists that we ask. James even tells us that we do not receive because we do not ask.

The Cheyenne church to which we ministered was dependent. I now realize that we made it that way. Our stated goal was to develop a mature church under native leadership but, "They are not ready yet," we always said. Very slowly we came to understand that the church must be given responsibility if it was to take responsibility. It had to make its own mistakes and learn from them just as we had.

We were short of men in the church. There had been some strong leaders in the congregation, nearly 40 years old then. One of them was murdered; others drifted away. We prayed. We tried to be specific. We asked for five new men in the church, and God gave us five. Our faith was too small. We should have asked for 20. Raccoon, Bear Standing in the Shade, Walks on the Ground, Twenty Stands and Other Coyote became Christians.

Neso'eoeve (Twenty Stands), was stocky, friendly, bilingual, literate. We usually spoke English with him and called him by his English name. He had the marks of a leader. His wife had been a Christian for a number of years before he joined the church.

We became friends, and he was often in our home. We celebrated birthdays together. He taught us many things about the Cheyenne language and Cheyenne customs. He told us Cheyenne stories and jokes.

Cheyenne humor, we found out, often poked fun either at the teller of the joke himself or at a brother-in-law. If there was a brother-in-law around, you were more or less obligated to tell a ridiculous story about him.

Occasionally the humor had a bit of a bite to it, like this joke from *Nahkoheso* (Little Bear), Pastor Joe Walks Along. "When the white people landed on the moon, that was a real disappointment. I thought maybe they were trying to find a new place to live so they could return this country to the Indians, but all they did was bring back a few rocks."

I took one of my rare hunting trips with Twenty Stands. We didn't bring home a deer but he showed me where to find fossilized snailshells on the top of a high hill, and I really enjoyed being with him. He took over responsibility for the weather station I had been keeping as a volunteer for the Weather Bureau. He helped me write Cheyenne sermons. We talked often together about community needs, housing, alcohol treatment, jobs. Were there ways we could cooperate with each other in improving our houses?

He moved his house near the church, "to get away," he said, "from some of the bad influences that surround us in the Cheyenne village." The children's Sunday School was taught in English and that seemed to be a good place for him to pitch in. He was willing, clever, and quick, and became a regular teacher.

Another of the five men who became Christians at that time was *Ho'evahtamenestse* (Walks on the Ground), whom we knew in English as Stamper White. Pastor Alfred Habegger of Bethany Mennonite Church in Busby, known in Cheyenne as *Haa'ese Oxhasestse* (From Far Away), asked me to teach Walks on the Ground in preparation for baptism. Walks on the Ground spoke only a little English. We had a catechism in the Cheyenne language prepared on the traditional European model with questions based on a logical outline of Christian beliefs answered by selected Scripture verses.

I could tell that Walks on the Ground was not getting much out of our study together. Between my stumbling, elementary grasp of the Cheyenne language and my method of teaching that was utterly foreign to him, not much was happening. But Walks on the Ground was patient with me. If this was what you had to do to become a Christian, he was going to do it.

After his baptism he surprised me by asking if we could study the Bible together. "Where do you want to begin?" I asked, thinking we might read some of the stories in the Gospels. "Let's start with Noah," he responded. For a month we read and reread this story in the Cheyenne language. It wasn't so

Walks on the Ground studying.

much that Walks on the Ground read the material, it was more that he memorized it as we read together. Then he asked, "What does it mean?" There were more weeks of study and discussion as we struggled with that question together.

A couple of months later, Christians from the four Mennonite Cheyenne churches gathered at Birney for a fellowship meeting. Both Twenty Stands and Walks On The Ground were there. After a meal together, there was an informal worship service in which any of the Christians were invited to speak or sing. Walks on the Ground now felt ready to share. He told the story of Noah, and applied it to the Creator's concerns about us. Twenty Stands also spoke, but I was disappointed. In contrast to Walks on the Ground his words seemed glib.

My reaction to Twenty Stands' sharing added to other nagging anxieties about him. In spite of our frequent contact, there was a kind of surface quality to our relationship. He could preach and teach, but the message was not always clear. Were we hearing what he really thought, what directed his life?

In contrast, Walks on the Ground and *Nahkoxhoveo'eoo'estse* (Bear Standing in the Shade), Oliver Risingsun, became the kind of people others turned to in times of trouble or fear. Without needing to be elected to a church office, both became acknowledged as elders in the church in Busby, White River Cheyenne Mennonite Church, as it was later known.

In Twenty Stands' extended family, it was said, there were medicine men. One uncle was especially feared because of his power to curse a person and bring sickness or disaster. Cheyennes were very careful around such a person. After one Thanksgiving Day, Twenty Stands told us that his relatives had gathered for a feast but he and his family had not been invited. That hurt. Evidently, because of his activities in the church, he had been rejected. He no longer belonged. It was getting costly to follow the Jesus road.

Arthritis slowly crippled Twenty Stands' wife. There were hints that he was being pulled in other directions. One night in late fall Esther got in the car and started for the village on an errand. Suddenly, she became aware that Twenty Stands had been hiding in the back seat of the car. It became clear that he was attracted to her.

Esther cannot remember just what she said, and Twenty Stands left without touching her, but we became aware that she was in danger. She does remember the gnawing ache and diarrhea she experienced in our last two years at Busby as her body reacted to these (and other) tensions. In times of foreboding fear, she found strength in prayer. "I felt God's protecting arm around me," she said, "I trusted God's armor to shield me."

Not long after these events, we were gathered in the living room for our family Christmas celebration with our children. The Christmas program and other activities in the church were finished and outdoor lights were turned off, when there was an insistent knock on the door. Twenty Stands stood there, agitated. He said that he had to talk to us. We closed the door to the living room, where the children were waiting for us, and sat down to talk.

He said that Satan had appeared to him as a very attractive, well-dressed person and offered him anything he wanted, including wealth, power and women. He was in conflict about this. He told us that Esther was included in the gifts that Satan had offered him. He made no apology for that.

We took his openness in sharing this with us as a cry for help. We talked for a long time. We looked together at such scriptures as II Corinthians 11:14 where we are warned that Satan can appear as if he were an angel of light, at I Peter 5:9 that describes him as a roaring lion hungry to kill us, and at Ephesians 6, where we are offered God's armor against the Devil's "evil tricks" and "burning arrows." We prayed together for God's help and protection.

Gone were the days when we could be at ease with Twenty Stands, as we once had been. Our hopes for him were fading. Disappointment set in.

Then came even more painful news. Twenty Stands had left his wife—now crippled with arthritis—for another woman. Alcohol was gaining a grip on him. We were told that he had been drunkenly arguing in Jim Town bar about what a great preacher they had in the Mennonite church in Busby.

In a bitterly ironic twist, Twenty Stands' second wife, too, became severely crippled with arthritis. They separated. Illness came to him, too. A stepson and wife cared for the dying father. The house he had abandoned when he left his first wife burned down, and with it the pictures and treasures of years.

As I think back on Twenty Stands' life, I wonder: did you, my brother, exchange the joy of flying, of catching the yellow moon, for a hollow promise that turned to ashes? Tears sting our eyes as the smoke wafts into a moonless sky now beyond reach.

He has sent me to bind up the brokenhearted,
to proclaim freedom for the captives
and release from darkness for the prisoners...
to bestow on them a crown of beauty instead of ashes,
the oil of gladness instead of mourning,
and a garment of praise instead of a spirit of despair...
Isaiah 61:1-3.

Chapter 7

Behind the Mission Station—To a Young Man

As if uprooted from a poplar grove,
tall and supple, I watched as you walked,
your hair black as a vein of Montana coal,
your skin brown and rose like the earth
shining in the bright sun.

And I, crowned like the wild yellow rose bush,
my body crossed with the white and pink of the peony,
my eyes with the hue of bluebells
lapping the Big Sky sun.

How is it that we drink the same air,
wake to the spiteful voice of the crow,
play under the same night star?

I crave your grace, the darkness of your hair.
You dance in my mind and color my heart.
I gather your startled young kiss
in my believing.

The pine trees raised us, the mountains,
the cold springs, the sand hills and sage.
What did we learn from these Old Ones?

I folded up my dream for you one day.
I saw too much had faded.
No use screaming and no use dying—
I shut my eyes to the summers of green,
of berries, and frogs in the creek.

The sun and moon have changed seats many times
and now I return to my starting,
to reclaim the memory—
red and yellow buffalo berries,
the scent of mountain air,
lovely tender days when I craved
the darkness of your hair.

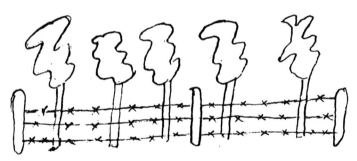

The "Crow row" behind the Corral.

⌐ Coal Mining and Assault Weapons

A wild yell shattered the quiet murmur of night sounds in the sleeping camp. It was 4:00 am. Cheyenne Christians had gathered for their annual Family Camp in a grove of Ponderosa pines near Crazy Head Springs east of Lame Deer. The yell had come from somewhere on the ridge above the camp, and it only added to a feeling of tension already in the air. No doubt that was its purpose.

The day before, the morning breeze had brought with it an ominous sound of gunfire. This was not the sharp crack of a Cheyenne hunter harvesting venison to feed his family. It was the heavier pounding of automatic assault weapons. The sound was coming from a spot less than a mile east, where the American Indian Movement (AIM) had set up camp.

Family Camp was a special time to come away for a while for fellowship and fun, learning and worship. It was a time to soak in the beauty of the world, to brush off for a few hours the persistent problems of life, and provide space to listen to the Creator's voice. But this year political events refused to be pushed aside.

Shoulderblade tent at family camp.

The Cheyenne Christians had always made it clear that non-Cheyenne Christian brothers and sisters were welcome to join them for Family Camp. This year several had responded to their invitation, some from considerable distances. The Cheyenne Christians and their guests would be together for four days, with the camp climaxing in a worship service and feast on Sunday. Funds had been raised in advance so that noon and evening meals could be offered free to all who came.

The day we heard the gunfire, a delegation of AIM leaders came to Family Camp and privately confronted pastor Joe Walks Along, asking why he and the Cheyenne Christians with him were consorting with the enemy, the white man. It had to be stopped, or else.... Pastor Joe shared the incident with some of the Christian leaders as a concern for prayer, but decided not to talk about it publicly to the campers.

Only a little over a year had passed since months of gunfire between AIM, the FBI and Federal marshals at Wounded Knee, South Dakota, had left dead on both sides. Some of the AIM people were Vietnam veterans, well trained in the arts of death courtesy of the United States military.

Now AIM had announced that they had come to help the Cheyennes in their negotiations with the energy companies. The cash-strapped Northern Cheyenne tribe, with the encouragement of the Bureau of Indian Affairs and the Department of the Interior, had signed contracts to permit coal mining and oil exploration on the reservation, only to realize later that the contracts would involve a virtual takeover of the Northern Cheyenne reservation by outsiders. The contract required the companies to set aside funds to ensure the restoration of land after strip-mining, but the amount—75 cents an acre—was a dirty joke. The contracts had to be changed.

The Cheyenne tribal council, we learned, had told AIM that they were welcome on the reservation but that the Cheyenne would use their own methods in dealing with the energy companies. AIM accused the tribal police, whom they saw as collaborators, of harassment. We were told that tribal leaders had instructed the police to avoid any possible confrontation with AIM.

Lawyers hired by the tribe discovered more than 30 violations of law in the way the energy contracts with the tribe had been drawn up. In a brilliant legal move, the Cheyennes confronted the Secretary of the Interior (who as trustee for the Indians had approved the illegal contracts), asking that the contracts be voided and new contracts negotiated to the satisfaction of the Cheyennes. After a month or more of pondering, the Secretary of Interior backed the Cheyennes, and the matter was settled without a protracted and prohibitively expensive legal battle. The energy companies did not even try to renegotiate. They knew that their contracts had been unfair.

On a later visit to Lame Deer we quite accidentally ran into the man who gave the yell that had awakened the camp. We had stopped to see *Hestaneoo'e* (In-the-Course-of-the-Wind Woman), an old neighbor. We found her in the Shoulderblade Center, a care home the tribal housing authority had built. Her son—the man in question— was with her, helping her eat her lunch, since her hands were so crippled by arthritis that she could no longer handle a spoon. How strong he looked! His expression showed that he had tasted much of life since those boyhood days in Busby.

We had hoped for much from this young man. His mother was a woman of faith, and her illness had not destroyed her trust in Christ. His father had shown potential for leadership in the Christian church. But the time came when we had to say of him, as the apostle Paul did of one of his potential leaders, "Demas has forsaken me, having loved this present world." We knew the son had been influenced more by his father's life than by his mother's faith.

As we tried to fill in what had happened during the many years since we had met the son, he tested us. He assured us that he had been trained to kill, even with his bare hands. He said he had to be careful when he was partying because it would be so easy to kill someone who angered him. He just had to walk away. Since his time with the military, he had traveled and also worked as a bodyguard for a rock singer.

Was this the same person who had blown out his birthday candles at our table and attended Sunday School with our children? We noticed how gently he helped his mother eat her lunch.

Yes, he had been a member of AIM. He was the one who had been training other AIM members to use the military weapons that we had heard during Family Camp. He was the one who had been standing armed guard that night. Armed guard against what, we wondered? Had there been other unseen guardians keeping watch over the camp that he knew nothing about?

He began to be more at ease with us. The AIM movement was "trendy," he admitted. He told us of his travels to Cuba to sample communism. Even though democracy had not treated his people well, he apparently found communism "trendy" too.

He and a few of his friends had gone out into the hills to fast and pray in the way of the traditional Cheyenne vision quest. For some, this was the way to gain a spirit helper in the form of an animal or bird that would ensure power and direction in dealing with life. He was a bit tentative in telling of this experience. He gave the impression that he and his friends had been experimenters rather than true believers. Not much seems to have happened.

The tension continued to drain from our conversation. We were hearing more clearly a person searching for a secure rock on which to build his life. This gave an opening to tell of the powerful spirit, the Holy Spirit, that we looked to for power and direction for our lives. We felt free to talk about the Creator's coming among us to point us to a new path, a path that would face the problems of the world with the power of love, rather than the power of a gun.

Although by then we knew that we could not determine the outcome of such a conversation, yet like gardeners spotting a tiny green leaf from seed presumed dead, we were startled and delighted later to receive a Christmas greeting from the young man.

> Therefore if anyone is in Christ,
> he is a new creation,
> the old has gone,
> the new has come!
> All this is from God...."
> *2 Corinthians 5:17-18*

The God of new beginnings!

Chapter 8

Picnic in the Forest

Standing on the Ice Well
I love to feel that coolness
slithering round me
on a hot, dry, August day.

The pines are all dressed
and sheltering a small feast
of wild strawberries.

Children playing and grown-ups talking
echoing through the valley.

I'm swirling through
yesterday's whispers
and today's voices

The mystery of mountains,
of sunshine cascading
through the wings of the pines.

Growing Rocks, Owls and the Ice Well

Cheyennes speak about a rock as if it were a living thing. I once asked Walks on the Ground why this was so. "Haven't you noticed that rocks grow?" he asked me. I was reminded of fields where farmers have to collect stones that keep showing up (growing?) in their fields. Some fields have so many that the farmer builds a large pile or perhaps a fence of stones along the edge of the field.

Walks on the Ground assured me that the hills and the mountains, the *ma'xehohonaeo'o*, or "great rocks" also grow. He pointed to a large red hill about eight miles northeast of Busby. Some mornings one could look down the Rosebud Valley and see that this hill would seem higher or larger than usual. The *ma'heono* (spirits or powers) lived in such hills, as well as in springs and rivers, he told me.

My mind went to my childhood home on the Snake River plains of Idaho. In the distance, about 30 miles north, were the eroded remains of ancient volcanoes standing on the otherwise flat plain. Buttes, we called them. There were times, usually in the early morning, when mysterious things happened to the buttes. They grew in size. A butte that usually could hardly be seen over the horizon would loom above the plain. Their shape might be distorted.

One memorable morning a huge cliff formed between the buttes. It appeared to be hundreds of feet high, a vertical wall like one side of a yawning canyon cut by a river, except that the fissures of the rocks appeared to be vertical. It created an seemingly impassable barrier in what had been a level plain between Big Butte and Twin Buttes. I watched for a long time until in the middle of the cliff the rocks began to fade and an opening appeared through which one could see the sky. Gradually the cliff melted away, the buttes settled down, and everything looked normal again.

I was given a name for this strange happening, a "mirage." It had to do with warm and cool layers of air near the ground. Perhaps so, but to me it remains a mysterious part of this strange and beautiful world. The Cheyennes saw a spirit world behind such mysteries.

The Cheyenne people also had a great deal of respect for the electricity loosed in the great bolts of lightning during summer thunderstorms. More than respect, it was often fear. High Hawk told how his grandmother explained that it was the Thunderbird that caused the noise and was responsible for the lightning.

I remember *Hanoseeeotse* (Dives Backwards) musing about another mystery. "There is a man speaking in Billings, and through this *nemenestotse* (singer) we can hear him right here in our house in Busby," he said. I felt a bit superior. I, of course, knew all about radios. Or did I? As I thought about it I had to admit that about all I really knew about radio waves and electricity was how to turn on the switch. Electricity is actually as mysterious to me as the growing hill was to Walks on the Ground.

While visiting our daughter Rebecca many years later in the innovative hospital in Goshen, Indiana, where she worked as a nurse, I noticed a picture of an owl on the wall. I immediately thought how worrisome or even frightening this might be to a Cheyenne child. The owl with its stealthy flight is called *ve'kesehemestaa'e* (ghost bird), and its presence is an omen of death.

I remembered talking late one night to Pastor Little Bear (Joe Walks Along). He took me to the window of his beautiful new house and looked out at the pole-mounted security light in the back yard. "An owl," he said, "has been perching there at night. The dogs bark when it comes but I haven't told the family because I do not want to alarm them."

Certain places also had an aura of mystery about them. One such place was our family's favorite picnic spot. Our family enjoyed picnics. They were a break from the telephone and the knocks on the door of our house. They gave us a bit of private space to be family. Our spirits were renewed as we experienced the silence, and absorbed the beauties and mysteries of creation. Sometimes we went with friends or took unexpected guests out into the hills for a meal. It was special when we could stay until darkness fell and tell stories around a campfire.

We often went to a place in the hills between Lame Deer and Ashland. There among the scattered Ponderosa pines near the bottom of a stream valley was what appeared to be an abandoned mine shaft, a relic of the white man's unrelenting search for gold or other mineral wealth. It was a hole about five or six feet across, lined with old planks, and surrounded by the piles of red shale that had been dug out.

We did not know how deep the shaft was, because about six feet down it was blocked by ice. Even in the 100° F heat of August, the ice remained. Cheyennes called this mysterious place the "Ice Well." In spite of the noise of the picnic, one felt a kind of hush in this place.

Each time science "discovers" more about how this world of ours functions, new mysteries are found below, beyond or above the new knowledge. Look at the sensitivity of plants to gravity: stems grow up, roots grow down. We may be able to give a name to the hormones responsible, and note how tiny an amount is required, "like a needle in a 22-ton haystack," as one plant physiologist calculated, but mysteries remain. We may know that the genes contained in each cell are the source of the myriad tissues that make up a plant—root, shoot, fruit, flower, seed—not to mention the greater complexity that forms a human being. But many details of how all this is controlled are unknown. To speak of the One who planned it all as the Great Mystery seems appropriate.

Even though through Jesus we can say that we "know" God, yet, unfathomed mysteries remain.

Psalmist to God

You created every part of me;
You put me together in my mother's womb.

I praise you because you are to be feared;
All you do is strange and wonderful.

I know it with all my heart.
Psalm 139:13-14, (Today's English Version)

God to Job

Can you raise your voice to the clouds
and cover yourself with a flood of water?
Do you send the lightning bolts on their way?
Do they report to you, "Here we are?"
Who endowed the heart with wisdom
or gave understanding to the mind?
Who has the wisdom to count the clouds?
Who can tip over the water jars of the heavens
when the dust becomes hard
and the clods of earth stick together?
Job 38:34-37

Chapter 9

You Picked Me Out

You picked me out,
white and blond.

I'm your spittin' can.
You're not quite in.

I'm out.

God, why did you
birth me blond?

I'm paying because
I'm white.

You're paying because
there's too much
shadow on your heart.

Squeeze your own
resentments into rage.

Move through the grayness.
Let your soul burn.
See the darkness,
admit the shadow.

I bow before the healer's
scarred hand, broken.

You see, I can't
pay two prices.

I can't even pay my own.

Asthma and Theft

"Am I going to live?" Esther wondered. Asthma had throttled her. Every breath became a hard, painful effort. What was so automatic it could be ignored was now obviously crucial to life—a breath away from eternity.

A calm hand and a little red pill eased the terror and the fear. Never mind the racing heart, at least breath was coming. With our doctor 50 miles away, we kept even more powerful and dangerous medications in reserve.

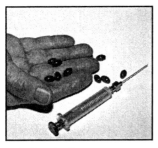

Little red pills.

Returning to our home late one night we found pumpkin pudding splashed on the walls of our kitchen. Checking to see what else the intruders might have done we discovered that some heirlooms, a watch and a necklace, asthma medicine—the little red pills—and some less important items were missing. Coal dust tracked through the house led us to the basement window—the point of entry. The tracks indicated that the burglars were not adults. This was the only time in the 16 years we lived at Busby that our house was broken into. We didn't even lock in the early years, until alcohol abuse made it necessary.

We were especially concerned about the missing medicine. An overdose might be life-threatening to a child. We informed the school and they discovered two boys passing out the little red "candies" to their friends. The school informed the tribal police.

The younger of the two boys involved, whom we will call Jim, had been abandoned by his mother. His father's occasional drunkenness did not help. He was being raised by his grandmother, who brought him to Sunday School. Jim once vented his anger by taking his father's tools and burying them. The older of the two boys was a neighbor who had lost his father, shot to death by a policeman in an off-reservation town, we were told. The family felt there had been no good reason for the shooting. Apparently there had been no investigation. The victim, after all, was an Indian. This boy had been in trouble before.

The Cheyenne tribal police asked for a list of stolen items. We had not intended to get the police involved but we provided the list and asked that they notify us if the boys were brought before the tribal judge.

Jim had been a special problem for our daughter Ann in school. As the only blond non-Indian in the classroom she was a convenient target for resentments against the white man or life in general. Jim especially targeted Ann and looked for any chance to punch her in the stomach after school or even after church. A neighbor girl decided that Ann had had enough and "beat up" Jim after school. This seemed to help.

About a week later, Jim's father stopped me to ask what had happened to Jim. I did not know. I had heard nothing. I finally learned that he had been picked up by the police on his way to school, taken 100 miles to Billings for a trial in federal court and had already been sentenced to reform school.

Apparently someone had placed a dollar value on the things stolen from us that passed the arbitrary boundary between misdemeanor and felony. Tribal courts could not handle felony cases. They were transferred to federal courts. Not one of the Jim's relatives had been informed! We had not been informed! We checked with the relatives of the other boy and discovered that they had not been notified either. No friend or family member had been with the boys in court.

I was really angry. If this was our justice system, some changes were badly needed. I drove over to Jim's father's house and asked him to come with me to Billings. We were going to talk to that judge! We rushed off on the 100-mile drive without an appointment.

Amazingly, the judge consented to meet with us. He listened carefully but noncommittally and then left us sitting, wondering if we had wasted our time. To our surprise he returned and told us that there would be a new hearing, which we and other concerned people could attend, and that he would listen to hear any recommendations that we wanted to make concerning the boys. Apparently the court had not been adequately informed about the home situations of the boys and had decided that no one cared about them.

This was Jim's first brush with the law. I felt that sending him to reform school might make things worse. If we could get him in a caring home it might give him a fresh start. A Christian school teacher and his wife who were interested in Jim offered to take him into their home in another community as soon as school was out a month later.

A week later we were in court, and this time Jim's father and the other boy's mother were present. I was given the opportunity to explain about the family that was willing to take in Jim. The prosecuting attorney asked where Jim would be kept until the end of school. I hadn't thought about that, so on the spur of the moment I offered to keep him in our home. The judge agreed. Because of his previous record, the older boy was sent to reform school.

I hadn't thought this through very well. To our daughter Ann, this was like bringing her enemy under our roof. It left her with a sense of being betrayed by her own father. Jim was kept out of reform school, but the cost was greater than I realized. Can a father be so involved in his ministry that he forgets the needs of his own family?

However, Jim seemed to be on his best behavior. He ate anything we offered him, especially if he could put ketchup on it. He even polished his shoes, although his friends teased him about it. At the end of the month he was placed in the teacher's home.

Years later, when we were invited back to attend the Mennonite Family Camp on the reservation, I was surprised to see Jim at the Sunday feast. He kept to himself, so after I got my buffalo steaks and fry bread, I went over and ate with him on the ground in the shade of a pickup truck.

I learned that he had joined the Marines during the Vietnam War. He was trained for intelligence work and learned much about radios, computers and other communications gear. He was now on the staff of Dull Knife College in Lame Deer. Jim said nothing about the experiences we had shared during his boyhood, but it seemed to us that he had chosen to be at the camp so he could meet us again.

Chapter 10

A Death is Heard

Hear your brown soul
   muttering some small chatter.

Trying to say it doesn't
   matter.
Push and pull to raise
   the meaning.

You must call the old women
   to wail and cut their wrists.
They'll bring this rite of agony
   to your eyes and teach its fullness.

When you hear out this dying,
   the women will laugh and you will shine.

Bird Woman (Mary Redwoman) mourns her son's death.

Joan

No you can't visit her; it's after hours!"

The nurse at the Indian Hospital that served the Crow and Cheyenne people at Crow Agency was adamant. No matter that my wife Esther and I had been in Billings that day and were just returning from the nearly 200-mile round trip with 27 miles of gravel road to go. No matter that the patient we wanted to see was scheduled for surgery early the next morning. No matter that I was the pastor of her church.

Finally the nurse relented slightly. "I'll call her to the window and you can talk to her there."

The "window" was a small rectangular opening through the wall where one stood and stated one's business when entering the hospital. There would be no opportunity to place a comforting hand on our friend's shoulder. Soon *Eve'hanahe'e* (Eats About Woman), appeared in the window, her long black hair flowing over shoulders clothed in a hospital gown.

She was delighted to see us and began asking about the preparations for Easter in the church. "How did the practice for the speaking choir go?" She was part of the group that was to tell the story of Jesus' death and resurrection in a choral reading. Our services were usually a mixture of English and Cheyenne. As one of the early Cheyenne high school graduates she spoke and read English well. We usually called her by her English name, Joan Limpy.

We searched Joan's face for signs of fear or anxiety. Her mother, *Hahnomahe'hehe* (Wasp Woman), was strong on traditional Cheyenne ways. When Joan learned about germs in school she had asked her mother, who we knew as Hattie Limpy, if they could use separate cups for drinking. Her mother

Joan

answered derisively in Cheyenne, "Do you think you are so much better than we are that you can no longer use the common dipper to drink from the water bucket as we always do?"

I wondered if the mother had been reluctant to trust her daughter to the white medicine man who said he would cut out the pain in her stomach. For some Cheyenne people the hospital was a place one went to die. The white man's medicine was often used as a last resort and many did die there.

There were no hints of worry in Joan's face. As we later drove home through the darkness, Esther asked, "Did you see a special glow in Joan's face?"

I had noticed the same thing. In place of the expected anxiety, her face was peaceful, in fact almost joyful. Years later I saw something similar on the face of one of our daughters during her wedding. Since Joan did not talk about the imminent surgery, we gently asked what her feelings were. She made it very clear that she had placed herself in the hands of God, and whether the outcome was life or death did not really matter.

It had not always been that way for Joan. We had rejoiced when she and three of her friends had declared their willingness to follow Christ and were baptized at the Bethany Mennonite Church. Her mother had previously been baptized, as were most of her sisters, one of whom was a deaf mute. Her father, *Mo'eohtooveotse* (Elk Shaking Itself), was dead.

When Joan was growing up, her mother did not always have a house. They spent at least one winter in a tent with a stove in it. I do not recall how cold it got that winter but I know that the snow was nearly a foot deep and most winters it got down to -20° or -30° F on the coldest nights. There was a lot of wood to cut and the stove had to be tended night and day.

Even though she had Christian family members around her it soon became evident that things were not going well with Joan's Christian life. She attended church only sporadically. Often she avoided us; she obviously did not want to talk to us. She married a man who was not a Christian. He proved to be so abusive that his mother counseled Joan to leave him to protect herself and their baby. She did, but then there was another baby by another man who showed no interest in helping her raise their daughter. And other young men....

In some ways Joan's life was all too typical of what was happening to the Cheyenne people. Once noted for their chastity, their marriage relationships were now getting so tangled that we started keeping notebooks to help us remember how people were related to each other.

We left Busby for a year to attend seminary, and when we returned I remember meeting Joan in the Busby store. Immediately my eye caught something different about her. There was an openness that signaled something new. She did not look away, but responded to my greeting.

Gradually we learned her story. In summer Joan and her mother and children often moved a few miles up Rosebud Creek to live among the plum bushes and red rock hills on land that her mother owned. Here she had time to be alone, and here God had met her. She became sure of His love and presence in her life. All things became new. She was no longer available to the young men who had been taking advantage of her, even hiding in the bushes or rocks until they left. Her mother, Wasp Woman, hinted that the changes in Joan's life were almost more than she could handle. It was soon obvious to the entire community; Joan was a new person.

She began attending church regularly, bringing her own children and often her neighbors' children with her. She expressed a willingness to train to become a Sunday School teacher. She enrolled in an adult winter Bible School. But most of all her life had direction. She now wanted to live for the glory of God. We watched with awe at what God was doing.

Then the periods of sharp pain struck her. The Indian Health Service doctors decided that the Joan's problem was gallstones, and scheduled an operation.

The next day the news came. As the surgeons were finishing a routine operation, Joan's heart had suddenly stopped. They opened her chest and managed to massage her heart back into action, but her brain had been deprived of blood dangerously long. She lingered for a time and then died.

We, relatives, friends, Christians, gathered to mourn. Death had come among us just as we were preparing to commemorate Jesus' death on the cross. We tried to look beyond our pain, beyond the questions that had no answers, to the resurrection for hope in our darkness. Why?

At funerals, which came far too often to our little church, I usually managed to keep a kind of emotional distance from death, even tragic death. I could be the outside observer of the culture of Cheyenne burial customs. But not this time. Joan was family, a sister in the Lord. God, how could you have snatched her from us? My tears flowed. Esther and I decided to remember her by giving one of our daughters the middle name Joan.

> Consider now! Call for the wailing women to come,
>> send for the most skillful of them.
> Let them come quickly and wail over us
>> till our eyes overflow with tears
>> and water streams from our eyelids...
> Teach your daughters how to wail;
>> teach one another a lament.
> Death has climbed in through our windows
>> and has entered our fortresses;
>> it has cut off the children from the streets
>> and the young men from the public squares.
> *Jeremiah 9:17-18, 20-21.*

Summon the mourners, begin the healing!

Chapter 11

You Were Thirty

You were thirty; I was ten.
You had been to prison.
I hadn't been much of anywhere.

You smelled like leather
hair grease, too few baths,
and hitchin' in the sun.

Your brown arms tightened
as you tooled designs into
leather in that old cabin.

I watched your dark eyes.
Sometimes you played your
guitar while I listened.

I heard a song today that
played so much like one
you would have done.

I got to thinking
about that day you left
and didn't say good-bye.

And the devil showered you
in booze and metal and fire.

And you didn't say good-bye.

▙ "Ernie" and the Butcher Knife

The Indian police stopped by. Did we know Ernie? Yes we did. Did we have a picture of him? We did.

Cheyenne Policeman.

Ernie (not his real name) had been in and out of our home many times. We had talked together, eaten together, worked together, prayed together.

We knew only a little of Ernie's childhood in Birney. The only relative he ever mentioned was an aunt who lived there. We had learned not to ask too many questions about the past in a place where confusion and despair often left tragedy in its path. We do not remember his Cheyenne name; to us he was just Ernie.

Ernie did tell us many stories of his adventures in far-off places—

"Ernie" drawing.

California, Washington. About his heroic rescue of a person trapped in a fire. About a marriage—or was it a marriage?—to a white woman. The stories were sketchy, with details missing. We wondered how he had made a living. There was something painful about that time that he didn't care to talk about, as if telling would result in rejection. Some of his stories left doubt in our minds.... Had this stuff really happened? Or was he trying to impress us? To deal with some of the hurts of the past? To prove something? Had he lived through all that? We never knew for sure.

We did know that he had learned to manipulate people. How else could he have survived his lonely journeys in the white man's world? Though internally we remained wary, we also sensed that he was hungry for love and friendship, and we tried to reach out to him despite our suspicions.

We had talked with Ernie about the Christian faith. The Cheyenne word for Christian is *E'oestaahe* (water-put-on-the-head person). We preferred the way the Cheyenne gospel songs described the Christian life as "walking on the Jesus road."

Ernie by now had become quite active in the Mennonite Church. He played guitar and drew sketches to enliven the primers we made to help people learn to read Cheyenne. When we Christians tried to imagine what Jesus' birth might have been like had he come among the Cheyenne, Ernie portrayed Joseph welcoming the wise ones in feather headdresses who had come to his borrowed tipi to worship his son, the new-born chief.

Cheyenne version of the Christmas Program.

Ernie had helped out with the children's clubs, showing kids how to tool designs into leather and do other crafts. We made it possible for him to get some additional leather-working tools so he could make some things for sale. I still have the key case he gave me, with a cross etched in front of the tipi, the Bible on the other side.

Our attempts at friendship didn't always succeed. Watching Ernie sitting on our living room couch, I began to feel that he was showing undue interest in one of our daughters who was sitting next to him. I no longer remember what I said. I am sure I tried to conceal my anxiety, but he saw through it immediately. Anger welled within and he left without a word, but within an hour he was back, his tongue loosened by liquor, to express his hate against the white man's prejudice and pride, his power and privilege.

Late one summer night Ernie stopped by our house. We talked in the darkness. He wasn't drunk, but something like drunkenness had hold of him. I began to realize that it was hate. He told me that he was on his way to kill Crying Hawk. As I tried to find out why, I heard only confused answers. He showed me the butcher knife he was carrying. I tried to talk him out of his evil plan. I asked him to leave the knife with me, but nothing I said moved him. He stalked off into the darkness, the knife gripped in his fist.

What should I do? I doubted that I could successfully intervene physically. The police were 17 miles away and if we could get in touch with them it might be all over with before they could get there. Why had Ernie told me? Esther and I got on our knees to pray (which we didn't usually do) and told God we were helpless. We asked God to stop Ernie's murderous rage.

In about an hour Ernie was back, the knife still gripped in his hand. He was trembling, half-sobbing, and saying over and over, "I couldn't do it. I couldn't do it." He said he had raised his arm but he couldn't drive the knife home. We were awed. Ernie gave the knife to me and we finally slept.

A while later Ernie left again on one of his journeys to faraway places. Months passed.

Then came the day that the Cheyenne police came around for a picture of Ernie. The Butte, Montana, police were trying to identify a body found in their city. We gave them a picture. We waited for word. None came. The Cheyenne police heard nothing. Ernie's aunt heard nothing. Ernie never came back.

Chapter 12

Porch Sitting

I was small then,
The porch was dark green,
with vines on a trellis.

You painted the sky evening
with a thunderstorm.

Pinks and gold
and deepest purple,
you danced in that rainbow.

I knew,
because some bottomless hole
set me longing.

I watched
this beauty,
like a branding of your name.

How can I be without you?
Yet I am.

▄ Dreams, Visions and Denominations

How can one be acutely aware of the beauty of creation and yet feel alienated from the one who created that beauty?

In my Bible School training I had been taught a kind of short-hand summary of how a person becomes a Christian. First you had to recognize that you were a sinner in need of forgiveness. Next, you had to believe the good news that Jesus had died to save you from your sins, and finally, you had to accept Jesus as your Savior and receive his forgiveness.

But now I was living among a people who did not have a specific word for "sin" in their language. You could talk about "evil," which might be anything from illness to a tornado, from murder to a curse put upon you by a person of power, or even something as common-place as tripping over a tree branch. There were spiritual powers that one should fear and placate, or learn to control, but "sin" as a concept was not a part of Cheyenne thinking. About the nearest thing we could get to sin was to talk about "doing evil." I was some-what disoriented. Was the summary of the gospel I had learned un-clear to the Cheyenne people? What then would be the "good news" that would attract them to Jesus?

Busby sky.

(KEN VOTH PHOTO)

Christians from some of the tribes where Mennonite churches are located (from such places as Cross Lake, Manitoba; Bacavi, Arizona; Porcupine, South Dakota; and Hammon, Oklahoma) had gathered in Lame Deer. They were meeting for fellowship along with some non-Indian brothers and sisters. Since not all of us knew each other, we introduced ourselves by responding to the question, "How did it happen that you said 'Yes' to Jesus?"

Jeremiah Ross, Cree pastor, told us through an interpreter about the time when he was working on his trap line in frozen Northern Manitoba, far from his home village of Cross Lake. He became deathly ill and went into a coma. He dreamed that he crossed a dark abyss and came into a place of light where he met a person to whom he was tremendously attracted. It was good there and he wanted to stay, but this person said, "No, you will need to go back because I have work for you to do there."

Jeremiah recovered from his illness and returned from his trap line trying to understand the meaning of this dream. For a long time he told no one about it. Although he was not then a Christian, he finally asked Ernie Sawatsky, a Mennonite Christian and church planter living in his community, to explain the dream to him. After some thought, Ernie suggested that it might be best to tell the people of his community what he had experienced, and ask them about its meaning. Jeremiah did this and the response was something like, "God wants you to be a Christian leader among your people." And that is what happened. He became a pastor of the local Mennonite church.

Walks on the Ground, a Cheyenne elder, told how he had been a member of the Peyote Eaters, and had also had a dream while sick in the hospital. In his dream he had seen his peyote brothers wandering lost and aimless. As a result of this dream he began to follow the Jesus road.

The Sioux couple, Ted and Mamie Standingelk from South Dakota, told how they had both become addicted to alcohol. In a dream they had seen a Bible verse just as if they were looking at a page in the Bible. The message of this verse was used by God as a step in freeing them from their addiction, and led to a pastoral and teaching ministry to their Lakota people.

Hearing these stories, I was driven back to the gospels to see how the good news was expressed in Jesus' encounters with people. I noticed that sometimes he simply gave the invitation "follow me," which sounded a little like the "I have work for you to do," that Jeremiah Ross heard in his vision. To the puzzled disciples who wanted to know where Jesus was going he said, "I am the way." And Walks on the Ground found purpose and direction that gave new meaning to the rest of his life.

All attempts to restrain the demon that possessed the homeless Gerasene man had been futile until Jesus said, "Come out of this man, you evil spirit." And the Standingelks could resonate with Jesus' claim, "If the Son sets you free you will be free indeed."

None of those who spoke had described their encounter with Jesus in terms of sin, repentance and forgiveness, yet these were surely involved. They no longer had their backs turned to Jesus but had come into vital contact with him. They knew that he was the creator who had come among us. The loneliness of alienation from God was eased.

I was among a people more aware of the supernatural than I had ever been. Rocks, trees and hills were the dwelling places of the *ma'heono* (the spirits, the gods). They had to be placated by gifts so that life would be good. When we climbed the hill across Rosebud Creek north of our home at Busby we discovered an *oestoono* (prayer cloths), an offering of many folded layers held down by five stones. Someone had given this expensive gift to the spirits living in that hill, possibly to gain power, healing or other favors, or to ward off their hostility. Ceremonies with complex rituals, fasting, dancing, even self-torture, would renew life. Cheyennes feared making mistakes in carrying out the ceremonies, which would render them ineffective.

When I first watched the ceremony of renewal the white people called the "Sun Dance," I did not know enough Cheyenne to understand what was being said. My colleague Pastor Habegger, then fluent in Cheyenne, told me how the priests prayed to the *ma'heono*, asking for mercy if they had blundered in any way in carrying out the ceremony. The Christians had adopted the singular of the word for spirits, *Ma'heo'o*, to speak about God in the Cheyenne language. Note how carefully *Ma'seeota'e* (Red Medicine Woman), whom we usually called Maude Fightingbear, defines the word in her song, "My God is the Most High":

> My God is the Most High
> He is the Truth and the Light.
> He sits as chief in the highest heaven.
> He has power and glory.
>
> My God is truly the one to be thanked.
> Because he is merciful and lovingly kind.
> My God is truly alive.
> He is the one who gave us eternal life.[19]

There was no lack of religion among the Cheyenne. They were surrounded by religion and religious influences. In addition to the Sun Dance there were other ceremonies such as the renewal of the sacred arrows. In 1894, about four years after the Mennonites had started their work among the Southern Cheyenne and the Arapaho, the Catholics arrived on the Northern Cheyenne reservation. As noted above, in 1898 a Southern Cheyenne had introduced a new Indian religion, the peyote "road." When Mennonite Missionary Rodolphe Petter visited the Northern Cheyenne in that same year, his ability to speak Cheyenne caused quite a stir, and some Northern Cheyennes asked him to bring the message to them in their own language as well. Mennonites started their work at Busby where the Catholics did not yet have a church, but ultimately we were competing in all four Cheyenne communities.

Preparing for the Sun Dance.

Ho'evotse, John Teeth, my neighbor, whom I sometimes hired to bring a dry log for firewood down from the hills with his team and wagon, stopped in to talk one day. After a while he got around to the question that was really bothering him: "Why do you Christians fight each other?" The question embarrassed me. Were we really fighting? Were we not warning people of dangerous misunderstandings of the gospel on the part of some Christians? Were we not defending the truth?

Or perhaps we *were* fighting each other. I remembered how angry I had been when I found out that the priest had invited children from families that we considered "ours" to his after-school classes, and then baptized them, apparently without parental consent. My attitude was evidently reciprocated. The children reported that they found out how the Mennonites had gotten the Bible: they had stolen it from the Catholics.

The picture was further complicated when Crow Indian Christians introduced an indigenous form of Pentecostalism, resulting in three churches that did not always acknowledge each other as full brothers and sisters. Then the Mormons built a church in Lame Deer and sent many young people into Mormon homes to attend school in other states. (We Mennonites also had done some of this, but had realized that it often did more harm than good.) A Lutheran church was established near Muddy Creek, followed by the Southern Baptists in Lame Deer and Ashland, not to mention the Jehovah's Witnesses, the Seventh Day Adventists, and others who made efforts to promote their points of view on the reservation.

John Teeth did not live to see all of these religious groups arrive, but he asked the right question. How could the Cheyennes find their way amid this confusion of voices? How could the Christian gospel become at home in Cheyenne life and culture?

High Hawk's father, Bear Standing in the Shade, had become a Christian through the healing and later the death of his younger son. Since he had previously been a follower of the Peyote road, High Hawk asked him, "You have been on both sides of this, you have been a peyote eater and a Christian, what do you see as the difference between the two?" His father said he would think about that. A day or two later he answered his son's question, "In Jesus I found life."

In John's Gospel, Martha was faced with the terror and mystery of death in the loss of her brother Lazarus and was upset by Jesus' puzzling delay in coming to help until it was too late. Jesus presented himself to her as "The resurrection and the life." Then he demonstrated his power over death, and Lazarus lived again.

Bear Standing in the Shade had seen something of that power in Jesus. His son Orlup was sick with dropsy, his body swollen, bedding wet, doctors unable to help. Christians prayed. When his father returned from busing boarding school students home for the weekend, Orlup called, "Dad, come here." Anxiously the father went to the bedside. Orlup said, "Look," and threw back the covers. The swelling was gone. "Get my clothes, I want to go out and play." This convinced Bear Standing in the Shade to begin walking the Jesus road.

When some time later Orlup's sickness returned and he died, his father said, "When Orlup was healed I opened the door and put one foot in. Now [with his death] I step inside and close the door behind me."

I asked our daughter Ann what she meant in the closing verse of "Porch Sitting":

> This beauty like a branding of your name.
> How can I be without you?
> Yet I am.

She said, "This is about all the religion I had around me. I found beauty painful. Alongside the sunset I saw hardened cracked mud with beer cans lying on it; snow splattered with blood. Beauty and death. The storm made me wonder, who is this God? I am not close to this God."

In the cemetery.

Chapter 13

Tall as a Barn

Tall as a barn,
wide as a cow trough,

wild like a forest fire,
you're pregnant with whisky.

I watch the town
emptying toward me.

I hear the fear
as it washes before you.

The shades are pulled down—
women cowering.

Now you're standing there drunk;
Dad's out there looking calm.

I've heard the stories.
This isn't the first time
you've emptied town.

Daddy said you were a lamb,
that you walked home willingly.

But as for me,
I knew you were big enough
to have killed him.

I didn't know much
about angels then.

▃ Two Birds Is Drunk

When *Ve'keseo'ohnešese* (Two Birds) was drunk, people said, five men couldn't pin him to the ground. They were afraid of him. He had more strength than he should have had. Did some powerful spirit possess him when he was drunk?

Thinking of Two Birds, who we knew as Pete Little Bear, took my mind back to a particular Halloween night. One white man's custom that Cheyenne youth had adopted with relish was Halloween "trick or treats." It wasn't so much the treats they wanted, it was the tricks that were fun. These usually included toppling the church's outhouses, ringing the church bell in the early hours of the morning, and other mischief.

Those outhouses were well-built, heavy structures, and getting them set up again required organizing a work party. In those days when alcohol was just beginning to spread its tentacles throughout our community we seldom locked any doors. But on Halloween we dug out the church key and locked the door. I also did some patrolling to minimize the work we would have to do the next day.

As I came out of the moon-cast shadows in back of the church, it was obvious our locks had not accomplished much. Here were Two Birds and some of his buddies standing by an open window of the church pulling on a lariat rope that disappeared into the darkness. They vanished as I arrived and I discovered that they had somehow entered the church, tied their rope to the bell rope and threaded it through a window so that when the bell sounded across the community they could make a quick escape. I returned the lariat to Two Birds later in the week. I still chuckle at their ingenuity.

So many things changed as alcohol increasingly crept through the community, especially after the soldiers came back from World War II. The military had been very liberal in providing alcoholic drinks, and drinking, soldiers had discovered, temporarily blocked out the terrible things some of them had experienced. Now Cheyennes were using liquor to erase, at least for a time, some of the nagging pains that living on a reservation at the pleasure of the white man still caused. The loss of the old freedoms, of land, buffalo, chastity, language, music, medical knowledge, identity, purpose, direction, manhood, brought on an aching grief. The numbness of alcohol provided help to deal with this loss.

The former security of the community was broken. If a car stalled along the road it was best not to leave it for even a few hours lest the battery, tires, and wheels disappear. Anything that might be sold or traded for drinks was at risk. We began locking our doors. Alcohol is a hard master. It demands a loyalty that takes precedence over all other loyalties.

We had a good relationships with Two Birds, although he was not a churchgoer. Once the west side of the church roof, damaged by hail, needed reshingling. The Christians discussed this and some volunteered to help. We were out on the roof getting started when Two Birds unexpectedly showed up. I finally realized that he was not just there to watch but had come to help. He worked with us until the job was done.

I suppose Two Birds had reasons to drink. He had been in the military. His wife had abandoned him, leaving a small son that the grandmother was doing her best to raise. But alcohol becomes its own reason. One Sunday morning the grandmother brought the boy to Sunday School. One of the first things he did was to pick up some of the new pencils we had just purchased from the church's meager resources and break them in half. What kind of meanness was this? Some time later we learned that his father had been on a drunk Saturday night and that the grandmother and the boy had spent the night in our barn seeking shelter from Two Bird's violence. I was ashamed that she had not felt free enough to ask for the protection of our home.

One Palm Sunday morning, low gray clouds curtained off the sun, but 30 or 40 Cheyenne people had gathered to remember Jesus' donkey ride into Jerusalem through the cheering crowds. It began to snow during our service and the nearby houses of Busby village could no longer be seen. As we walked out of church there was already two or three inches of snow on the ground and the wind was picking up. We were used to snow, but it didn't usually come this fast.

We took some of the older people home in our car. It did not take long to realize that we were in for a blizzard. Normally we had an evening service, but as the storm continued we decided it would not pay to heat the church again, as no one would be out on a night like this.

It snowed and blew for two days. We didn't go anywhere. Roads were blocked. We learned later that the local highway department snowplow had run into a huge drift of wet snow about a mile out of town and turned over. We never knew exactly how much snow fell in the storm because the wind had blown it all into drifts. We guessed that it had been almost two feet. By bringing in rotary equipment from the more mountainous parts of Montana the Highway Department finally got the highway open by Maundy Thursday.

After the roads were open, I met Two Birds at the store. He chided me, "Why weren't you at the church last Sunday night? I came over through the blizzard and there was no one there. Where were you?" I was startled. Why had he tried to come to church when he knew that no one would be there? Or had he come *because* he knew no one else would be there? Was there something he was trying to get up the courage to talk about? Our home was only a few yards from the church. Perhaps he was just teasing me.

One warm, bright summer afternoon a group of women and children came hurrying to our house. They were frightened and looking for help. "Two Birds is drunk," they said. They anxiously lowered the shades of our living room so no one peering through the window could see them. *"He'kotoo'e!*, Sit quietly!" they warned the children and the children obeyed.

The children's instant obedience reminded me that it once had been essential to survival on the plains to teach children to be absolutely quiet lest they reveal their presence to an enemy. Even babies could be kept from crying. Raiding parties had vanished into history, but there was not a sound in our living room that day.

Soon I saw Two Birds walking unsteadily toward our house. I decided it would be better to meet him outside rather than letting him come to the door. He wanted to know where the women were. I tried to divert him by talking about other things. He wanted to wrestle with me. I politely declined. We talked some more. I asked if he would like to go to his home. He wasn't interested. Standing on the lawn in the shade of the big cottonwood tree I kept talking with him. Again I suggested he might want to go home. He wanted to wrestle. More talk. Finally he agreed to go, but only if I would go with him.

So we started off. He put his arm around my neck. We staggered on. Then he wanted to sing. So we sang. I'm glad there weren't any video cameras around in those days—just a few frightened people peeking from a darkened room.

Chapter 14

Reservation Bar, "Jim Town"

There's a place just a few miles from here,
   behind which tavern
   sculpted in the sun
   are mountains of
      bottles
      and
      cans.

Cans whispering tales, bottles exhaling stories,
   frozen men,
   feet skating in blood,
   jaws broken,
   bodies crushed in metal,
   children's shoes sold for booze,

      cans,
      bottles
      and
      cans.

"White Man's Water"

A young couple was standing by their car in front of our house. He was very angry and unsteady on his feet. Suddenly, with a wild swing, he drove his fist toward her jaw. She moved quickly enough so that he struck the side of the car instead and broke his hand.

Once before, we knew, she had not been quick enough, and the doctor had had to wire her jaw shut for several weeks while the broken bone healed. We remembered her utter frustration while living on fluids. She finally convinced the doctor to remove the wires earlier than he thought best.

These two were what passed for a "successful" Cheyenne couple. They were educated, had well-paying jobs, a better-than-average home, beautiful children. He could afford to drive 110 miles to Billings for a haircut. Yet his addiction to alcohol was slowly but inexorably destroying their marriage.

At times there was not enough to eat in their house, and we tried to help out. Sometimes she and her children took shelter in our home. I can still hear his little dark-haired, dark-eyed girl explaining as she came through our door, "My daddy's drunk!" When a car horn honked in our yard at 5 am, the mother rushed out to quiet her husband before he woke our whole household. The pain was so deep that drinking Lysol or shaving lotion to blot it out was not unthinkable.

One night we heard a timid knock at our back door. Bent over, completely worn out, the woman entered. With great weariness, in a blank, flat voice she told us the latest chapter in the unending saga. We talked for a long time. We ourselves understood only poorly what steps might be taken to begin to deal with the addiction. But we could listen, pray, offer a glimpse of hope in the darkness.

Finally she told us that she had been carrying a rifle with which she planned to kill herself. It was now propped by our back steps.

She allowed us to keep the rifle temporarily when at last she returned home.

Early Cheyenne leaders knew all too well how *ve'ho'emahpe* (white man's water) had been used to defraud and debauch their people. They had supported the law that made it illegal to sell liquor to Indians or to bring it onto the reservation.

But times had changed. Younger Cheyennes and other Indians began to interpret the laws against selling liquor to Indians as discrimination. Just as some restaurants would not serve Indians, and some hotels refused to accommodate them, they couldn't buy liquor like a white man. This resulted in political pressure on the federal government to repeal the restriction against selling liquor to Indians.

The Northern Cheyenne retained the prohibition on the reservation but it proved almost unenforceable. It was only four miles from Lame Deer to the reservation boundary, and Jim Town Bar was the first building you saw across the line. The time would come when, according to a tribal official, about 90 percent of the work of the Cheyenne police and courts involved liquor violations.

At first it was mostly the men who had been in the army who drank. But soon wives gave up the struggle and joined their hus-

Cans and bottles behind "Jim Town" Bar.   *(DON DILLER PHOTO)*

bands. We held funeral after funeral after funeral. The old ones began to ask, "Who is going to be left to raise the kids?"

My own experience with alcohol had been extremely limited. I had my first taste of alcohol when I was 10 or 12 years old. My mother had found a quart of home-canned cherries that had spoiled. She asked my younger sister and me to take a taste of it, explaining that some of the cherry juice had turned to alcohol and she wanted us to know what it tasted like. We didn't want to. We had been taught that alcoholic drinks were to be avoided. But mother insisted, and we had our first sip of wine. I doubt that I had another taste until I shared in a communion service where wine was used years later.

I had heard a few stories about drunkenness in my youth—a neighbor once did considerable damage with an ax while drunk— but I had never seen a drunk until I was attending The Bible Institute of Los Angeles (Biola) and joined a group that tried to witness on skid row. There I began to see the dark side of alcohol in graphic detail. I am not sure that our witnessing helped anyone there, but we learned a lot.

So I didn't know much about alcoholism at first, but my friendship with Little Bear taught me much about the power of addiction. Little Bear had had a major drinking problem, but when he became a Christian he sobered up. His church helped him finish high school and attend Cook Christian Training School in Phoenix, Arizona. While at school the students visited churches of various denominations. As they prepared for a communion service in one church, Little Bear caught the scent of the wine they were using. Beads of sweat broke out on his forehead. Should he take the cup? Would it ignite that old desire for more drink that could sometimes hardly be denied? If he refused to participate in this part of the communion service what would these Christians think of him and of the Bible school that they were helping to support? He didn't want to bring shame on the name of the school.

The elders were approaching; he had to decide. He drank from the cup. Then the battle began. A raging thirst demanded more wine. A still, small voice reminded him that he belonged to Jesus and urged him to grasp the shield that would deflect the burning arrows of the evil one. All day the battle continued. In the end alcohol lost.

While we often felt helpless in the face of alcohol addiction, God had shown us that he could deliver from this terminal illness. One day a group of us were driving to a meeting of the district conference of our church. We stopped at a restaurant for breakfast. As we were studying the menu I said to Little Bear, "I think I'll have some pancakes. Are you going to have some too?" "I never eat them," Little Bear responded, "Ever since I was the 'guest' of the sheriff at Forsyth for a month and he fed us nothing but pancakes, I don't eat them."

Little Bear doubtless got his start drinking while a soldier in the Korean War and continued when he returned home. He remembers that when the sheriff arrested him and his buddy he had said, "I think we got the two worst drunks on the reservation."

Little Bear got sick while he was in jail. His buddy was in a

different cell but close enough so they could talk. He knew how sick and lonely his friend was. In an old, tattered Christmas issue of *Life* magazine he had discovered some familiar hymns and he sang some of them to encourage his friend. Little Bear started thinking about his life.

He told us that he had been very shy when he was young. As a boy he would rather walk to school along the creek than along the road

Little Bear (Joe Walks Along)
(MARTHA PLANK PHOTO)

where he would meet other people. Back from the war he did walk the road, which took him past the Mennonite church on his way to the store. He noticed that Pastor Habegger often seemed to be just getting his mail from the roadside box and wanting to talk to him just as he came by. Little Bear's buddies asked him, "Why do you let that 'holy talking white man' bother you? Why don't you just hit him in the nose?"

But Little Bear couldn't do that. He respected the pastor and felt that he cared. The Jesus road began to look inviting to Little Bear. He started to attend church. Once one of the Christians asked him to pray at the close of the service. His first impulse was to dash out the door and run, but he stayed and prayed. Finally, he was ready to say that he would follow the Jesus road and was baptized.

As Little Bear was getting started in his Christian life he needed to get a job. He applied to the Indian Health Service for work as an ambulance driver. He was required to list on his application every time he had been arrested and convicted. "I couldn't remember all that, the list would be as long as my arm," Little Bear said. So he went to the police station to get a copy of his records.

He discovered that they weren't there. A year or so earlier the Bureau of Indian Affairs had decided to combine the police forces on the Northern Cheyenne and Crow Indian reservations with a central office at Crow Agency, about 40 miles from Lame Deer or 60 from Ashland and Birney. Although the two reservations shared a common boundary, this proved unworkable, if for no other reason than because the Crow and the Cheyenne had been traditional enemies.

Little Bear discovered that in the transfer of police records to Crow Agency and back to Lame Deer his records had been lost. He felt that God had something to do with that. He was hired.

After the changes God had worked in his life, and after three years at Cook Christian Training School, the Mennonite Church in Lame Deer invited Little Bear to be their pastor, a position he has

now held for many years. He is now best known by his English
name, Joe Walks Along.

As Little Bear thinks about the amazing fact that "the worst
drunk on the reservation" has become a Christian pastor, he remem-
bers a bitterly cold night when he and his buddy were drinking in
Miles City, Montana. In order to avoid the police they took a little-
used ranch road on their way back to Lame Deer still 50 miles away.
The car hit a snowdrift and got stuck. His friend was driving, and in
the process of trying to get out of the drift, he burned out the clutch
on the car. Then he passed out.

Little Bear was still alert enough to know that if they did not get
to a warm place soon they would freeze to death. He managed to
wake his buddy, and they struggled back several miles on foot through
the darkness to the little town of Rosebud. There they went into the
small railroad station to warm up.

After they had warmed themselves a bit, they went back outside.
Where to go? The next town on the way home was Forsyth, 15 miles
down the highway. With below-zero temperatures and the wind blow-
ing, the chances of them making it were almost nil, but they started
out anyway.

Cars kept passing them, but suddenly one stopped. It was a
white rancher who invited them into his warm car. Little Bear now
feels that that could have been his last night if God had not had
something more important in mind for him.

> Act like people of good sense and not like fools.
> These are evil times, so make every minute count.
> Don't be stupid.
> Instead, find out what the Lord wants you to do.

Don't destroy yourself by getting drunk,
but let the Spirit fill your life.

When you meet together
sing psalms, hymns, and spiritual songs
as you praise the Lord with all your heart.
Always use the name of the Lord Jesus Christ
to thank God the Father for everything.
Ephesians 5:15-20 (Contemporary English Version)

Chapter 15

Evening

The smell of cigarette smoke
in the open air.

A smoldering of emotion
coming from somewhere

I know somebody's meeting,
two brown lovers bedding.

Who said what or where?
How do I know it?

There's this action somewhere,
but no trails there.

▌ On the Public Display of Emotions

"Sometimes I would wake at night worrying about my teenage daughter," *Mokee'e* (Little Woman) said. "One time I got up and drove 40 miles to try to find her." Things had been different when she was young, Little Woman (Louise Fisher) told us. If the young man who was courting her invited her to an event in another community, she was permitted to go, but her mother and younger brother rode along in the back seat. Her mother did not say anything or participate in the event, but patiently waited to return home with her daughter and suitor.

This motherly concern for daughters has a long and honorable history among the Cheyennes. For young Cheyenne men of the past, as John Stands In Timber tells it, courting had its problems. How did one avoid this protective watchfulness of Cheyenne mothers? They were with their daughters *all the time*, wherever they went, day or night. John explained, "You did not want the mother to know who was trying to visit the girl, so you went over and hid near the tipi or the house. When she came out by herself you would catch her and wrap her in your blanket and have a long conversation. Sometimes the old woman would come out and say, 'That's enough! Go on home!' and you didn't dare stay."[20]

George Bird Grinnell, a scholar who had contacts with the Cheyenne from 1870 on, and spent much time with them from the 1890s to the 1920s, reported: "The women of the Cheyennes are famous among all western tribes for their chastity. In old times it was most unusual for a girl to be seduced, and she who had yielded was

Cheyenne Girls.
(MARTHA PLANK PHOTO)

disgraced forever. The matter at once became known, and she was taunted with it wherever she went. It was never forgotten. No young man would marry her. This seems the more remarkable, since the Arapahoes, with whom the Cheyennes have been so long and so closely associated, are notorious for the looseness of their women."[21]

When we began to live among the Cheyenne in the 1940s many forces were chipping away at Cheyenne morality. The examples of white neighbors (at least as reported in community gossip), popular music, Hollywood movies and, later, television, presented and still presents a very different set of values to the Cheyenne people. Actions that would have been unheard of in the past were daily displayed. Cheyennes assumed a new set of morals that made personal pleasure the measure of behavior, rather than loyalty to, and a willingness to sacrifice for, the community.

A Cheyenne friend and I once were reminiscing about the 1960s. I told her about walking by the dormitory of the Tongue River Boarding School at Busby, where a second-floor window was wide open. From a record player balanced on the window sill, Elvis Presley was belting out, "You ain't nothin' but a houn' dog..." My friend finished the phrase, "cryin' all the time."

"Well you ain't never caught a rabbit/ and you ain't no friend of mine," the song went on to say. "When they said that you was high classed/ well that was just a big lie," and then repeated the rabbit refrain again.[22]

"That sounds to me like a put-down song," I told my Cheyenne friend. "Is that the way Cheyenne youth understood it?" I asked, thinking about how often they were told that their ways were inferior and should be replaced by the white man's ways. "Yes," she said, "That's why we got drunk."

But the boarding school itself was probably the single most destructive force eroding Cheyenne morals. It was designed to "civilize" (make white persons) out of the children. Keeping them away from parents, away from those watchful Cheyenne mothers and "aunts," was a part of the strategy. The results were predictable. Time-tested social boundaries were destroyed.

Accompanying a group of boarding school students to an evening church service, we had to be alert lest a couple slip off into the dark and the girl end up with "grass on her back," as the Cheyennes sometimes put it.

Married and unmarried relationships became so confused that we had a hard time sorting out who was related to whom. Illegitimate children were not particularly looked down upon in Cheyenne society, but the confusion of relationships did have its impact. Still, some men and women—the minority—remained true to each other during long married lives.

In the old Cheyenne way, it was not appropriate for men and women to make public shows of affection. I came from a background with similar ideas. My parents and their people had been very restrained in showing affection. I had not thought much about this until, after some years with the Cheyennes, I saw a young Cheyenne couple holding hands as they walked down the road. It startled me, and I realized that I had never seen this before.

Still bright in my memory is a scene from my boyhood. We were invited to my grandparents' house with other relatives to meet visitors from Ohio. When we arrived, the visiting wife was in the circle of conversation but the husband had been delayed for some reason. Later when he entered the door he walked immediately across the circle to give his wife a hug and a kiss before he turned to meet the rest of us. That was so different from my experience that I have remembered it ever since.

I had much to learn in expressing feelings. Our oldest daughter, Betsy, lived hundreds of miles away with her grandparents for her sixth grade school year. When we came to get her at the close of school I still remember how awkwardly I greeted her.

On recent visits to the White River Cheyenne Mennonite Church in Busby we have noted how the Christians embrace each other warmly after the service. This is such a change from the early days. I have learned that one of the effects of frequent use of alcohol is to block the expression of emotions. Treatment centers help people to express and deal with their feelings in appropriate ways rather than deadening them with alcohol. I wondered out loud whether this new way of expressing affection in the Christian family might have come in part from experiences in such treatment programs. Some agreed that this was the case.

In recent years the Cheyenne people have come to realize that a side effect of alcohol abuse is sexual abuse. They are beginning to work at holding people accountable for their acts. Our culture, with its obsession with sex, has not been helpful.

Bear Standing in the Shade once told his son High Hawk, "Don't worry that sometime you might discover someone in the community is really your half-brother or half-sister. There are none." Bear Standing in the Shade lived with his wife *Vonahe'e* (Medicine Bundle Woman) faithfully for 62 years.

Chapter 16

I Open the Door

I open the door.
You stand there
big as a bear,
eyes bloodshot,
vision blurred,
only half there.

I am acting like
it's all the same to me,
but I don't feel it.
I call for Dad.

I've lost my ringlets,
most of my hair,
my chubby face.
But I'm still wondering:
What's on that side
of the door?

High Hawk's Love Affair With Alcohol

High Hawk (Ted Risingsun)

When he talks about the years when alcohol dominated his life, High Hawk likes to tell about the time he conned us out of a bottle of rubbing alcohol. His "very painful shoulder" was actually a consuming desire for a drink, and if nothing else was available, rubbing alcohol would do. In our naiveté, we gave him some.

He has shared with me how that seemingly unstoppable desire distorts one's life. "I would lie to my best friend," he said. No other loyalty, not even to wife or children, was stronger than loyalty to the bottle. As he began to recover, he told us how he kept finding bottles he had hidden around his house to stave off the disaster of being separated from the most important thing in his life.

This helplessness was very real, and very hard to acknowledge. Yet deep down High Hawk realized what his addiction was doing to his life and to those he cared about. He felt shame, guilt and self-hatred. High Hawk's love affair with alcohol began when he served as a soldier in the Korean War. Deeply troubled by some of the unthinkable things he had to do, he found temporary help in the chemical forgetfulness of alcohol, but the helplessness and self-condemnation that followed also drove him to attempt to take his own life.

Some things about alcohol we learned by experience and observation. A request to use the bathroom in our home, we discovered, could result in a missing bottle of shaving lotion. If a friend's breath was overly fragrant it might be because he had drunk a bottle of lotion. Even young children who were over to bake cookies kept wanting to taste the vanilla. Some things were better kept hidden.

When Esther asked the fourth graders in her after-school Bible class at Birney, "Is there anyone you want to pray for?" she heard: "Yes for my dad, he got drunk." "For my mother, she got beat up." "For Alex and Jim [absent members of the class]. They always go drink what's left in the bottles and cans laying around." We heard of baby-sitters who would put a bit of alcohol in the milk bottle to "help" a baby get to sleep.

One winter night we were returning in a snowstorm from a shopping trip to Hardin when we came upon a stalled car about 20 miles from home. In it were *He'heeno* (Blackbird) and his wife and children, also returning from shopping. The car proved impossible to start, so we offered to squeeze the family into our car. Then perhaps Blackbird could come back and get the car in the morning. As we were transferring groceries into our trunk, I noticed that Black Bird was taking special care with a couple of boxes. Then I saw that the bottom one was a case of beer.

"Friend, Black Bird," I said to him, "you know that it is illegal to take beer onto the reservation. I cannot take that case of beer. Perhaps you could leave it in the trunk of your car or hide it in the bushes over there." But if the beer could not go, neither would he. So we finally took his family home and left him in the snow with his stranded car and his case of beer.

Our friend High Hawk taught us much. Unlike Little Bear, who had been delivered from alcohol when he became a Christian, High Hawk had periods of sobriety followed by utter failure. Sometimes he stayed sober for a year or more, testifying to the strength that God gave him. When alcohol again took control he was so ashamed that he did not want to be seen in church—or by his neighbors, for that matter.

When he was sober his Cheyenne people would call on him to help them with their political problems. He was largely responsible, for example, for getting the Busby school placed under tribal control. He was also very helpful in the tribe's successful battle to prevent energy companies from taking over much of the reservation for strip mining coal. He frequently flew to Washington, DC, and was on a first-name basis with some members of Congress.

In 1966 we left the reservation and moved to Newton, Kansas. For the 50th anniversary of his parents' marriage, High Hawk and his sisters asked us to come back for a special surprise celebration. A feast at the school and special meetings in the church were planned. We were in his sister's home after we arrived when High Hawk came in. He strode over, gripped my hand and said something like, "It's been four years and three months!"

At first I thought he was talking about how long it had been since we had seen him, but the dates didn't add up. Then I understood. He was telling me how long he had been sober. As we got into his almost-new blue car, he paused with his hand on the ignition switch and said, "God gave me this; every other car I have ever had I ruined while I was drinking. God gave me this one."

Later he told us the story. His drinking had been getting worse: he would start in the best bar in town and a week later end up on skid row. One binge started in Billings and ended in Ashland about 125 miles away. And he had no idea how he had gotten there!

One Sunday morning he was sobering up after a long drunk. He was alone in his house. His wife had left him long ago. The grandparents were raising his two girls. The living room floor was cluttered with empty bottles and cans. His mind was beginning to turn to thoughts of suicide, as it had during the Korean war years before. He knew that it was going to happen unless something intervened soon, but he felt absolutely helpless against the terrible drive to drink.

In his despair he cried out, "God, you've got to help me. I can't stop, I can't stop."

"There were no lights from heaven to indicate that God had heard me," High Hawk said. "I decided to try to clean up the trash in the living room."

Still weak from his binge, he had paused to rest and watch a bit of TV when several of his drinking buddies came to the door. "We're going to Hardin, do you want to go with us?" They hadn't said why they were going to Hardin, but he knew. "Sure, I'll go with you," he said. He explained that he just did not have the strength to say "no" to them. "OK," they said, "we'll come back and pick you up." They left, but somehow never made it back. Finally it dawned on High Hawk that God was helping him when he was helpless.

The next Friday a buddy dropped in. "I've got a check from that land sale in my pocket and I've just had a big fight with my wife. Come on, cousin, we're going to Sheridan, and we're going to paint the town red." By this time God had given High Hawk the strength to answer, "Sorry, you'll have to go by yourself, I can't go with you." Little by little God had been giving him the strength to say no.

One morning years later when we were living back in Busby for a few months, High Hawk and his friend *Vo'kaa'ohvovo'haestse* (Spotted Antelope), a Pentecostal preacher we knew as Sylvester Knows His Gun, came for a visit that lasted most of the day. They told us that they had spent a great deal of energy in the past helping their Cheyenne people with some of their economic and political struggles. But something was always missing. The solutions often did not solve much.

Now they had come to the conviction that the most important thing they could do for their people was to help them be reconciled with God through Jesus Christ, to be a forgiven people. They intended to make that the focus of their remaining years.

I do not think that we ever encountered Cheyennes who did what might be considered "social drinking." Drinking almost invariably led to drunkenness. The oppression that Cheyennes experienced made

the numbing effect of the drug tempting. Unless and until this de-
mon can be bound, much pain lies ahead for the Cheyenne people
and others who take the risky chance of befriending alcohol. What
joy to open the door and find there a brother or sister whom Jesus
has set free!

Number Eighteen of Thirty Wise Sayings

Who is always in trouble?
 Who argues and fights?
Who has cuts and bruises?
 Whose eyes are red?

Everyone who stays up late,
 having just one more drink.

Don't even look at that colorful stuff
 bubbling up in the glass!
It goes down so easily,
 but later it bites
 like a poisonous snake.

You will see weird things,
 and your mind
 will play tricks on you.

You will feel tossed about
   like someone trying to sleep
   on a ship in a storm.

You will be bruised all over,
   without even remembering
   how it all happened.

And you will lie awake asking,
   "When will morning come,
   so I can drink some more."
Proverbs 23:29-35 (Contemporary English Version)

Chapter 17

Feast

Mounds of golden fry bread,
covered with dish towels,
the smell of boiled meat.

Pots of coffee steaming
on the heating stove,
getting as black
as the sermon is long.

People seated on pews,
plates piled high,
this doggie bag tradition
of days gone by.

Kids running everywhere
in this two room church
in a town with a creek
and some log cabins.

They call this place
a reservation.
I guess there are reservations
about its existence.
A feast day is different,
all the grayness disappears,
the wind and snow turn to spring
in this little church.

Fry bread and boiled meat.

The Joy of Eating Together

We finally heard the story of how *Ma'eve'ese* (Red Bird) got the nickname *Vetseskevahonoo'o*, (Doughnuts). Long before our time, there had been a community feast among the Cheyenne people at Busby. At the feast, someone handed Red Bird a dish of doughnuts. Instead of taking one or two and passing it on around the circle, he ate the whole plateful. Till the day he died he was Doughnuts! Among the Cheyenne you were sure to hear about it if your actions did not measure up to expectations.

A carload of representatives of the Cheyenne Mennonite congregations was making the long day's drive to the annual meetings of the district conference. I was driving and was anxious to get there at least in time for the evening sessions, if not for supper. My Cheyenne companions were hungry and hinted that it was already supper time and we should stop to eat. But I drove on. Little Bear never let me forget it. Years later he would tell the story of when Malcolm was in too much of a hurry to eat, much to the amusement of his listeners.

The Cheyenne people understood the importance and the joy of eating together. Early photographs of Cheyenne church services show a great circle of people enjoying lunch together, even if at times there was little more than coffee and crackers. Some of the people had come miles by wagon, so the meal was important. The hitching rail for tying up horses still stood in front of the church at Busby when we arrived in 1944.

As transportation became easier, the weekly lunch at church was dropped, but always at Thanksgiving and sometimes on other occasions we enjoyed a feast. Teenagers came to help bake enough pumpkin pies so everyone would have a piece. The women brought large enamel pans piled with fry bread. A service of thanksgiving preceded the feast.

At the time the poem describes, the church had no indoor plumbing, no church kitchen, and no fellowship hall with tables, yet somehow 60 or 70 people enjoyed a meal together, sitting on the same benches they had occupied during the service. Food was precious: none was thrown away. If a child was full before her plate was empty, the leftovers went into the lard bucket the mother or grandmother had brought to take food home. A good feast in Cheyenne tradition must have more food than people could immediately eat. I often thought of the 12 baskets of leftovers after Jesus fed the 5,000 from a boy's lunch.

Once my wife and I were invited to a feast put on by a family to honor a milestone in a relative's life. There were people attending from the other end of the reservation that we did not know, and they apparently did not know us. Introductions were not commonly made. We were on our own in finding out who strangers were.

One of the ladies preparing the food set a bowl of *ame* on the table in front of us. A Cheyenne granny commented loudly in her own language, "Why did you put that *ame* in front of those white people? They don't eat that." Laughter erupted from those who knew us, first because they knew we had understood the comment, and also because they knew we considered *ame* good eating. This mixture of dried deer meat and berries pounded fine was once the ration usually carried by Cheyennes on the hunt or the warpath. Even now it was prized as a nutritious food.

Years ago we visited Bethel Mennonite Church, a Cheyenne congregation, then located in the country near Hammon, Oklahoma. At the end of the service Jenny Hart, wife of pastor Homer Hart, invited the entire congregation to a meal. Before anyone took food from the bountiful table set under shade trees in the churchyard, she explained that this meal was given in public acknowledgment and thanks to God for answered prayer and celebration of God's power in the healing of a very sick relative.

In recent years we were gladdened when after dire medical predictions of birth defects, and after much prayer, a grandson was born with apparently all he needs for a normal start in life. Our minds went back to Jenny Hart and the way she expressed her thanksgiving to God when prayers had been heard. We decided to invite our congregation in Newton, Kansas, to join us in eating together as we thanked God for his gift to us.

At the end of time, God is inviting all of us to his great feast, the "wedding supper of the Lamb." John, Christ's servant, saw an "enormous crowd...from every race, tribe, nation and language" (Blackfoot and Crow, Choctaw and Cree, Arapaho and Sioux, Navajo and Metis, Ojibway and Creek, to name just the tribes in Canada and the US where there are Mennonite churches). We look forward to sharing this happy feast with Cheyenne friends and those of other tribes, celebrating the union of God and his people and the creation of the new heaven and the new earth. Every time we eat can be a foreshadowing of that feast. (Revelation 9:9-12; 19:5-10)

> Say there! Is anyone thirsty?
> Come and drink—even if you have no money!
> Come, take your choice of wine and milk—it's all free.
> Why spend your money on foodstuffs that don't give you
>   strength?
> Why pay for groceries that don't do you any good?
> Listen and I'll tell you where to get good food
> that fattens up the soul!
> *Isaiah 55:1-2 (The Living Bible)*

Chapter 18

Divorce, Brown on Brown

The old moon returned.
I wanted it gone.
This curse taunts,
it laughs through my mind
and in some peoples faces.

Die, moon!
You're no use in this darkness.
We sit, my little one and I—
suspended.

He comes and goes
with his heavy bundles,
hating what he has done,
too proud to relight his smile.

We once stood together,
we once laughed and yelled,
our hair was very shiny.

He cuddled the little one,
made her a little hammock and smiled.
She swung above our bed.

Yesterday others noticed our strength.
Tonight sorrow
has pushed down our heads.

█ The VW Gave Up

I followed the sweeping downhill curve of the highway. It was a soggy Sunday morning, the windshield wiper pushing the rain aside. But I thought I must not be far from the reservation where I hoped to meet my friends, Larry and Barbara Martin (not their real names), and perhaps attend church with them.

With a sudden thud the engine on my VW "Bug" gave up. I let the car roll to the shoulder. There was no response from the starter. The fire had gone out, as the Cheyennes would say. I was stranded. How do you hitchhike in the rain?

I was on a trip visiting churches. I had met with a group in the city on Saturday and my next appointment was in a country church on Sunday afternoon. Since the reservation was on the way, I had hoped to stop and visit friends.

As I sat and wondered what to do next, I thought back on how I had come to know Barbara and Larry. Barbara Martin was a Cheyenne woman from Montana, whom we had known since she was a girl. She had been active in the church, was alert, and had potential for leadership. Her husband Larry was from another tribe and they were now living in his hometown.

Larry was a tease, a lot of fun. Our daughters loved him. Some years earlier, Barbara and Larry had surprised us by choosing to attend a Mennonite college in the town where we were then living. Asked to speak to a group in one of the local churches, Larry told them that he might be willing to paint his car bumpers black (as some Mennonites have done to avoid the flashy, prideful display of chrome), but one thing he would not give up was wearing a feather in his hair to remind him of his Indianness.

Barbara and Larry were often in our home. He took our daughters to visit an African-American congregation he enjoyed. We joined him there too. When our granddaughter was born in Mexico City, he memorialized the event by making a model of the hammocks that his people made for their babies. These hammocks were hung over the parents' bed to make it easy to rock the babies back to sleep at night. For his shop class he took one of our old end tables and brought it back superbly refinished. One of our daughters, a nurse, was present when Larry and Barbara's first child was born. After college they moved to his reservation.

Here I sat, so close, yet so far, from their home. I tried hitchhiking by watching the rearview mirror and sticking my thumb out for a ride whenever a car came along. There were few cars; it was, after all, Sunday morning. Finally a pickup truck stopped, and the driver offered to take me three miles to a little town just off the highway where I might get some help.

How could I get in touch with Larry and Barbara? The last time I visited they hadn't had a telephone. I remembered that in some Indian communities the local police will take a message if there is a special need. So I called the police and they agreed to deliver a message.

Time went by slowly and no help came. I was beginning to get anxious about getting to my afternoon meeting. The rain stopped so I decided to walk to the highway and try to hitchhike again, this time with no success, until at last a car appeared with Larry at the wheel.

He and Barbara had been at services in their church and had received a message that went something like, "One of your buddies is stranded at the next town down the highway and he wants you to come and get him." He had no idea which "buddy" he was looking for. For all he knew, it was someone who had spent Saturday night drinking was now afoot and needing a ride home. But he came.

When I had explained my dilemma to Larry, he told me I should take his car to the afternoon meeting. "I just bought it last week and it should be in good shape," he said. I was reluctant to do this because I knew they would need the car before I could bring it back.

"Could you take me to the city and see if I could rent a car there?" That was about 25 miles further down the highway. "Sure," he said, "and don't worry about the VW. I will see to it that it gets towed to my place."

I was able to rent a car, and after a quick restaurant meal we parted. I made it to my meeting, and when I returned the following week Larry met me at the bus and brought my suitcase that had been in the car. Later, when arrangements could be made to repair the VW, he made sure that it got towed into the city. I have warm feelings as I think about this experience. Larry treated me like a relative, and in the community of faith I was.

Over the years we occasionally heard news of Larry: he had been elected to the tribal council; then he became tribal chairman. In a community in which many live dysfunctional lives, people look to someone they can rely on to take leadership positions. We were happy for him, but also anxious. In the world of political power there are special pressures: Meetings to attend in distant cities; cocktail receptions; nights in hotels with the ever-present bar; sometimes, after a few drinks, bed hopping. Sadly, it was sometimes the people with power in the white man's world who modeled this behavior.

We hadn't heard much for a long time when the bitter news came: Larry had fathered a child by another woman while on one of these trips. Their marriage was on the rocks. We lived at a distance then. When we tried to visit, Larry did not want to see us. He seemed to feel that there was no way back. He stayed with the other woman. Barbara later remarried.

In the old Cheyenne way, divorce was possible. The woman (who owned the tipi) could set her husband's things outside as a public sign that he was no longer welcome. The man, for his part, could strike the drum at a public dance and announce that he was "throwing away" his wife or giving her to another man.

Since we believe it is the creator's intention that marriage be a lifetime commitment, Barbara and Larry's divorce was very hard on our family. We hardly knew how to relate to our friends in their pain. There seemed to be no path to healing. Had we failed in prayer? We saw Larry only once again when he spoke at a college. We keep in touch with Barbara, who continues to serve the Lord, but much that might have been has been lost.

In the poem that begins this chapter, Ann puts herself in Barbara's place and tries to express how it might feel when covenant is broken.

Chapter 19

Old Brown Woman

Old brown woman
   shawled against cold grayness.
The snows have come;
   the smell of wood smoke smarts in the air.
The camp is still
   except for the splitting of wood and the barking of dogs.

You back around the corner of the log cabin
   seeking a place to hide.
Your eyes cast down,
   and yet I know the crimes crying in them.
You were crushed
   and there is no cover for the nakedness.

Oh if you could know the Spirit
   who frees the bitterness to cry,
Who warms the tears for shedding,
   and teaches them not to grow older.

"They're Crazy"

An old lady, wrapped in a blanket, her head covered with a black kerchief, shuffled her moccasined feet in short quick steps toward our door. We were still very new in the Cheyenne community, but we knew her name—*Hao'hoeva'e*, Dora Littlehawk. She mounted the two steps of our log cabin home, tapped with her walking stick on the porch floor to announce her arrival, and then peered through the etched glass window of our front door to see if anyone was at home.

How were we going to handle a visit with Dora? We knew only a few words of Cheyenne and had never heard Dora say anything in English. Our co-workers, fluent in the language, were away. At least we could open the door and welcome her.

Dora Little Hawk holding Wenger baby.

As it turned out, there was no problem. As she came through the door, Dora started talking away in Cheyenne just as if we could understand every word. If we would listen, she would talk. She seated herself and arranged her several skirts. The wrinkles on her face became a friendly smile as she continued the rhythmical flow of Cheyenne words. As we soon found out, few others spoke the language with such clarity and beauty. This was a gift to us because, like children first learning to talk, we needed to learn the music and rhythm of the language even when the meaning still largely escaped us.

As our knowledge of Cheyenne improved, we discovered that Dora liked to tell stories of days long past, before the "Time of the Horse" and even before the "Time of the Buffalo," back to the years that the Cheyenne people called the "Time of the Dogs." They then lived in a forested area near much water (likely the Great Lakes).

Here they fished, hunted and did some gardening. Dora explained how the dogs helped the Cheyenne by carrying burdens on their backs. Later the Cheyenne developed the dog travois, two sticks fastened into a collar with the other ends dragging on the ground behind the dog. A small platform or net between the sticks in the back supported the load. With the travois a dog could carry much more than it could on its back alone, so hunting and moving became easier for the Cheyenne.

We began to look forward to Dora's visits. I can still hear the chuckle with which she punctuated her stories. She rejoiced with us in the birth of our first child, a daughter. One of our treasured pictures shows her holding our baby on her lap.

Some years later Dora came to our door carrying a bundle of blankets. We talked for a while and then she got to the point of her visit. Would we be willing to keep the blankets for her? Of course we would! But the request saddened us because we knew what was behind it. These blankets were a kind of bank account for Dora. If she was short on cash she could exchange a blanket for what she needed. Bringing them to our house to keep indicated that they were no longer safe in her own cabin. She could no longer trust her grandchildren.

One of the strengths of Cheyenne culture was respect for the old ones. The hunter who brought in his kill first offered some meat to the elderly who were no longer able to hunt. Elders were sought out for their knowledge, wisdom and advice. They were largely the ones who transmitted Cheyenne history, values and pride to the grandchildren.

Little Bear remembered how every evening his grandfather would tell stories to him and the other grandchildren before they went to sleep. They were expected to respond from time to time with *"he"* (we're still awake). Eventually, when there were no more responses, grandfather knew they were all asleep.

The Cheyenne people also felt that responsible positions should only go to people of experience and wisdom. Once I was talking to a southern Cheyenne man about taking a position of leadership in the church. His first reaction was, "I'm not old enough," though I was sure he was in his 50s. Rarely in the "Time of the Buffalo" were the young and inexperienced put into positions of leadership. (In surprising contrast to this, children were sometimes named as leaders of community events. It was understood, of course, that these were honorary positions and that their elders would see to it that the responsibilities were carried out, and it did nothing to change the conviction that age and experience were indispensable requirements for respected leadership.)

But now, in the "Time of the Reservation," respect for the elderly was eroding. The money and food stamps that the white man's welfare system gave to the elderly was somehow different than giving the old ones the first piece of meat from the hunt. The money came from the white man and was fair game for theft. Alcoholism only added to the problems.

Emasehaneeo'o, "they're crazy," was a comment we heard Cheyenne elders make many times about reservation youth. They somehow felt that their youth were out of control. Traditional Cheyenne ways of teaching and discipline were breaking down. Basketball, movies, TV, parties, and listening to records now filled evenings once used for storytelling by the elders. Where once the setting of the sun brought many activities to an end, electricity now extended the day. Youth stayed up late and failed to get up before the sun to take the long morning run that their elders had used to build up strength and stamina.

The whole fabric of communication between generations was breaking down. Youth were caught between two ways of life, with opposing values. Sharing with those in need was sometimes being replaced by snatching an elder's cash from its hiding place and catching a ride to the bar. Sometimes grandparents had to take on the full load of raising grandchildren. Where once it would have been unthinkable for the young to be disrespectful to their elders, now there were times when the elders fled for safety when their kids and grandkids came home drunk.

As Cheyenne values erode, some have suppressed the grief brought on by these losses with alcohol and drugs. Others have found that the warmth of God's forgiveness can heal the pain, melt the bitterness, and allow the tears to flow.[23]

> Since my youth, O God
> you have taught me,
> and to this day
> I declare your marvelous deeds.
>
> Even when I am old and gray
> do not forsake me, O God,
> till I declare your power
> to the next generation,
> Your might to all who are to come.
> *Psalm 71:17-18.*

Chapter 20

The Dark One Comes

It is a sunny Sunday,
   a summer day bright with green,
   the air warm.

The Dark One pounds the steps behind me
   like a sudden building
   of Montana thunderheads,
   rumbling threat to what was.

Suddenly this safe bedroom
   turns to storm,
   lashing out at me
   its lightning and thunder.

I am condemned to this unleashing
   of another's hating sky—
   hands and heart raining drops of rage;
   these winds of a violent carelessness
   falling all over my body.

Driven like a tumbleweed
   I'm now against the barbs
   of unknown fences.

There is no protection
   from the cold and the wet,
   drying into shame.

The night has come,
   the dying too of afterlight.

"Like a Tumbleweed Against the Barbs"

That Sunday left no special mark on my mind. Thinking back on it now I cannot distinguish it from other similar days. Was it a Sunday when Esther and I drove, as usual, to Birney for Sunday School and a service? Or was it one of the occasional times that we stayed in Lame Deer and participated in worship there? I do not remember. Fourteen years would pass before we would begin to understand what that Sunday meant to our daughter, Ann.

Ann was 16 years old, a capable, responsible young woman who had proven that in the absence of her parents, she could welcome unexpected guests, prepare a delicious meal for them, tell them something about our lives and community, and host them for the night.

Our family was then living in Lame Deer, Montana, the largest of the four Northern Cheyenne communities. It was a long, narrow town squeezed into the valley cut by Lame Deer Creek. On either side rose

Esther, Rebecca, Ann, Elizabeth and Malcolm Wenger. Grace, Martha (front).

grassy hills topped with clumps of Ponderosa pines. It is named after a Sioux chief who died in a battle with the US Cavalry near here before this land was set apart as a reservation for the Cheyenne people.

Here the tribe and the Bureau of Indian Affairs had their administrative offices. The Lame Deer Mennonite Church was led by Little Bear (Pastor Joe Walks Along) and his wife Victoria. We assisted in the work of this church but we also pastored the Birney Mennonite Church. Birney did not at that time have a resident pastor, although the work done by Daniel and Amy Schirmer, Hopi leaders, was still bearing fruit.

I always enjoyed the 20-mile drive over "the divide" from Lame Deer to Birney. Here and there along the creek Cheyenne homes were scattered. At places, large, whitish "sand rocks" loomed at the bottom of tan cliffs. These were remnants, we were told, of the bed of an ancient river that once flowed through this country. Where the earth was cut to make way for the road, red shale stood out against the gray-green of the grass and sage. Here at this bend in the road we once saw a lynx cat. Not far beyond is the cottonwood tree that blazes like a yellow torch in the fall.

Nearer Birney we sometimes stopped for a cooling drink of clear water at the spring that was piped to the roadside. Even in the driest of months, this spring kept flowing. Bushes nearby held bits of cloth as offerings. A short distance down the graveled road we passed the tree where the wild turkeys roost. There was also the curve where one winter the snowplow had left a false impression of solidity beyond the edge of the road and we were suddenly dumped in the ditch. What might have been a fatal accident, had it happened a few yards sooner, did not even require special help in getting back on the road.

Coming out of the hills into the valley of the Tongue River we began to see the village of Birney. The ridge of hills we had just crossed must have absorbed most of the scattered summer thundershowers, for the grass was usually dry and brown on the eastern slopes. Touches of green came from the cottonwoods along the river and a few fields irrigated with water from the river. The village of log homes had no post office or store—that was another nine miles upriver. In a white-frame church building we met with a small group of Christians, mostly women and children.

Often Esther and our youngest daughter came with me but our other four daughters would attend Sunday School and church at Lame Deer. Ann especially liked Virginia Toevs, an employee of the local general store, Lame Deer Trading, as a Sunday School teacher. Virginia had grown up on a farm near Alsen, North Dakota, a few miles from the Canadian border.

That Sunday Ann had walked across the yard from our house, the former parsonage, to the church. As people were visiting, waiting for the service to start, she realized that she had forgotten her Bible. So she ran quickly back home to her upstairs room to get it. Suddenly there were footsteps pounding on the stairs. A young man cornered her and tried to rape her. She managed to fight him off and he left.

Ann caught her breath, straightened her clothes and returned to the church service. Although we were usually in Birney on Sunday mornings, Ann thinks that we may have been in the service in Lame Deer that morning. She, however, decided not to say anything to us, in part because this young man was the son of dear friends of ours, a Christian couple who were often in our home. She didn't want to drive a wedge between us. Then too, she was not certain what might happen in the church if she made this public.

Later, when the parents of the young man were both sick at the same time, we cared for them and their two younger children in our home. It may have been at that time that the young man, although he was not staying with us, entered our home when all were sleeping and again attempted a rape. Ann managed to get him to leave by threatening to wake up the whole house.

Ann's attempt to tell a trusted Christian woman friend about the attacks led to nothing. Fourteen years passed and we were living in another community before Ann told us of these events.

> O Lord, hear my prayer,
>   listen to my cry for mercy;
> in your faithfulness and righteousness
>   come to my relief.
> Do not bring your servant into judgment,
>   for no one living is righteous before you.
>
> The enemy pursues me,
>   he crushes me to the ground;
> he makes me dwell in darkness
>   like those long dead.
> So my spirit grows faint within me;
>   my heart within me is dismayed.
>
> Answer me quickly, O Lord;
>   my spirit fails.
> Do not hide your face from me
>   or I will be like those who go down to the pit.
> Let the morning bring me word of your unfailing love,
>   for I have put my trust in you.
> Show me the way I should go,
>   for to you I lift up my soul.
>
> Rescue me from my enemies, O Lord,
>   for I hide myself in you.
> Teach me to do your will, for you are my God;
>   may your good Spirit lead me on level ground.
> *Psalm 143:1-4, 7-10*

Chapter 21

Always When I Had My Birthday

Always when I had my birthday,
the earth dried and flew in the air.
The lips of the grasses
cried for moisture.

My parched, cracked soul curled
with the leaves.
You were hiding.
My throat stayed dry and swollen.

The dry days brought the Big Fire.
The sky filled with smoke
and chaotic passion—
terror mixed in beauty.

I taste the dust,
feel my grubby skin.
I beg for a drop of rain,
for the fire to be contained.

The dryness within flames into terror,
chaos, passion,
torture in beauty, questions.

You seem so far away,
but if You stopped breathing
I would die and this dryness
would seem like torrents of water.

⌐ Fire!

A wisp of smoke rose from the dry grass near the pile where we emptied our cook stove ashes. It was not far from our woodshed, garage and shop, but was not yet visible from our house. The green grass of spring in the Montana hills and prairies sometimes lasts but a month or two before the heat of summer curls the leaves and dries the grass. Any spark might be the one that becomes a raging tower of smoke and flame devouring all it touches. Unchecked, the flames might travel for miles.

Driving along the road a couple of blocks from our house, the wary-eyed reservation forester spotted the smoke. Some quick work with a shovel, and the fire was out. Then he was at our door. Ashamed of our carelessness, we thanked him for stopping the blaze that might have taken not only our home, but others too. We also thanked God that he had passed by just at that moment when the fire could easily be put out. Fire—both man-made and natural—was a real and present danger in the dry-grass months.

Early in our stay at Busby we decided that the wall-supported chimney which had served for more than 40 years in our frame parsonage needed replacement. At some time in the past a flue had been attached to the chimney when a furnace was installed. As we tore down the old chimney the bricks came apart with hardly a blow from the hammer.

When we got down to the wooden bracket that had supported the chimney we were startled to discover that the wood around the furnace flue was charred. What had kept that house from burning down on one of those bitter cold winter nights when the furnace glowed red hot? (The record low for Busby was -52° F in 1936). Again we thanked God for his protection.

As we were coming home to Busby one hot summer afternoon a thundercloud darkened the sky to the west. Suddenly a bright slash of lightning struck among the grass and brush nearby. Immediately a

bloom of fire about the size of a car burst out and swiftly became a
range fire. Fortunately a shower followed the lightning strike and in a
few minutes the fire was out. But showers do not always follow light-
ning. In Montana, clouds sometimes unleash more lightning than
rain; start more fires than they put out.

Range and forest fires offered both danger and opportunity for

Forest fire.
(REBECCA VOTH PHOTO)

the young Cheyenne men who had
trained as fire fighters. It was uncer-
tain and dangerous work, sometimes
far from home. Twenty Stands told me
of the time his crew was flown into a
landing strip along a river in an iso-
lated Idaho canyon. From there they
would hike and climb miles to the fire.
As the plane approached the short, tree-
bordered landing strip, he saw wrecked
planes on both ends of the strip, and
wondered if they would make it in alive.

Another Cheyenne friend told me
that his crew was once trapped when a sudden wind change blew the
fire toward them. He flung himself down in a small clearing, his face
in the dirt for protection from the terrible heat, while the fire roared
by on all sides. Trained crews of Cheyennes and other tribes gained
a reputation as excellent fire fighters. They were in demand on diffi-
cult fires, and were well paid for their efforts.

I once watched the awesome power of a forest fire as it reached
the bottom of a tree-covered slope. Suddenly the fire "crowned," as
flames leaped to the treetops and literally exploded up the hillside.
Nothing could stop it. Firefighters had to choose another location
ahead of the fire and do the slow, hard work of building a fire line
that would deprive the fire of fuel at a place where sparks that blew
across the line could be extinguished.

I felt even more helpless the evening I looked out our east window and noticed flames coming out of the door of the community hall a block or so away. This was a large log building with a wooden roof. At that time the community had no water system, but the nearby school had a fire truck with a tank on it. By the time the truck finally got there, little could be done but to wet down the few nearby homes. Helpless, we watched the building burn. It was a spectacular sight. The fire feasted on the bone-dry logs and timbers. Breaking through the roof, the flames became a whirling tornado, hurling burning shingles high into the sky. Nothing was saved.

Community Hall

There were times when we felt as though forest fires had swept through our efforts to plant a church—a church that could be really Cheyenne and sustain its own life. Eaglefeathers, an early Christian and a really promising leader had been murdered. Another leader was drawn away by a religious group that had no permanent work on the reservation, and his influence was diminished. One of the first two ordained ministers abandoned the task. The other one, after years of faithful service, suffered a stroke while preaching and one side of his face sagged. (Cheyennes believed that this was the touch of a spirit punishing him for making a mistake in a religious ceremony.) A woman we had tried to train as a Sunday school teacher came to a tragic end. Her body was found by a roadside in New Mexico, an apparent victim of alcoholism.

In our last days in Lame Deer, before moving to a new assignment in 1966, a government official interviewed us in an attempt to find out why there were proportionally more teenage suicides on the Northern Cheyenne reservation than anywhere else in the country.

Shortly afterward, I spent most of a day with *Ho'honahkeso* (Little Stone), an adult who was threatening to kill himself. Sometimes, failure seemed the only reality. O God, where were you? Were you hiding?

One summer when we returned to Montana to participate in Family Camp, we heard that the weather had been unusually hot and that fires had threatened even the largest Cheyenne community of Lame Deer, but we were hardly prepared for the scene as we approached Crazy Head Springs. Where once beautiful green groves of pine had stood, only blackened skeletons remained. The burn had come within a hundred yards of the campsite, but the grove of trees that shaded the camp itself had been spared. Cheyenne Christians saw God's hand in this.

Family Camp was a time when Christian commitment was often declared or renewed. We were told of the occasion when a young Cheyenne father joined the group of people gathering in the growing dusk around the campfire for the evening gathering. He walked over to where a pastor was sitting and tapped him on the shoulder, beckoning him to come away from the group. By a tree in the darkness he told of his youthful excesses and of the need he now felt to commit his life to Jesus. They rejoined the circle. After the message by the visiting speaker, the worship leader, who happened to be the father of the young man, asked if anyone had something to say before they closed. His son said, "I do," and shared his decision with those present. There was much joy. This was truly holy ground.

Burn near Crazy Head Springs.

Returning to this place several years later we were gladdened to see hundreds of new trees already head tall or more, hiding the scar the fire had made. The forest was healing too.

> The poor and needy search for water
>> but there is none;
>> their tongues are parched with thirst.
> But I the LORD will answer them;
>> I the God of Israel, will not forsake them.
> I will make rivers flow on barren heights,
>> and springs within the valleys.
> I will turn the desert into pools of water,
>> and parched ground into springs.
>
> I will put in the desert
>> the cedar and the acacia,
>> the myrtle and the olive.
> I will set pines in the wasteland,
>> the fir and the cypress together,
> so that people may see and know,
>> may consider and understand,
> that the hand of the LORD has done this,
>> that the Holy One of Israel has created it.
> *Isaiah 41:17-20*
>
> Whenever I am greatly troubled
>> I pray to My God.
> Because He has said,
>> don't be upset and don't be afraid!
> Behold! I am with you
>> until the end of the world.
> —*Ma'secota'e (*Red Medicine Woman),
> Maude Fightingbear[24]

Chapter 22

Hotohke'e

My Indian name means star, Star Woman.
The sky where I was named is like
a sea of gold diamonds
held in angels' hands.

The brightness of the little ones
always touched me with silent awe.
Ma'seeota'e, Red Paint Woman,
gave me this name,
Star—diamond in the darkness.

Was I the first person you raped or the fourth?
Now your list is long, like the signature
of the Milky Way across the Montana night.

Your frontier—trying to snuff out the bright places,
penetrating with rage holy diamonds,
stealing another's place in the sky.

This old Indian woman and I
are going to give you a name, too:
Soul Snatcher.

⬛ Falling Star

The Cheyenne people dealt with some of the mysteries and enigmas of life with stories—myths usually told by grandparents around flickering campfires. Only at night could such stories be told. Listen to the story of *Hotohketana'otse* (Falling Star), condensed from the version told long ago to that recorder of Cheyenne tales, George Bird Grinnell.[25]

Two Cheyenne girls were lying outside the lodge looking at the stars. One said, "That star is pretty; I like that one." The other answered, "I like that other one better." Pointing to a very bright star the first girl said, "I like that star best of all; I would marry that star."

The next morning while gathering wood they saw a porcupine up in a tree. "I'll climb up and pull him down," said the girl who had chosen the bright star. She climbed the tree but the porcupine was always just out of reach. As she kept trying, the tree itself seemed to grow. Her friend called out, "Come down, this tree is growing taller!" "No, I can almost reach him now," she answered, and kept climbing. Her friend ran back to camp and told the people. They rushed out to the tree, but the girl could not be seen.

The tree grew and grew. At last the girl stepped off its branches and walked away from it in another land. There she met a middle-aged man who asked her to come with him. She was frightened and began to cry. "Why, what is the matter? Only last night you were wishing to marry me." He was the bright star. He married the girl.

When she went out to dig roots with the other women, he told her there was a certain kind of root with a great green top that she must not dig. To dig it was against the medicine. Daily she dug roots but wondered why the one was forbidden. One day she decided to dig one up anyway. It took a long time. When she pulled up the root she saw that it made a hole through the ground on which she was standing. She looked down through the hole and far below saw the great camp from which she had come. As she looked at the lodges and the people walking about, she became homesick and wondered how she could get down.

Nearby grew long grass and she began to braid it into a rope. After many days of work she had a great long rope. Placing a strong stick over the hole, she tied the rope to it and began to let herself down. Alas, the rope was too short. She held on, crying, but at last had to let go. The fall killed her but not her unborn child. He was made of stone; the fall did not kill him.

Honoxease, a meadowlark, found the child and took into its nest. The boy child grew rapidly and followed the little birds around as they began to fly. The time came when meadowlark said to him, "Son, you must go home now; there will be hard weather here. We are going to the south country. Your people live down by the stream." "I will go if you make me a bow and arrows," he replied. So the meadowlark pulled out some of its own quills and made four arrows and a bow for him.

Traveling for some time, he reached the camp and entered the nearest lodge where an old woman lived. "Grandmother," the boy said, "I want a drink of water." "It is very hard to get water," she answered. "Only the fastest runners can have water. There is a fearful monster in the water, a *mehne*, that draws to itself people who go near it." The boy said, "Give me your buffalo pouch bucket and your buffalo horn ladle. I will go for water." "But grandson," she said, "Many young men have been killed going for water, I fear you will be killed too."

He went to the stream and began to dip water. When the pouch was filled, suddenly the monster raised its head from the water and sucked the boy in. There he saw all the people that it had swallowed. Taking out his knife, he cut a hole in the monster's side and let all the people out. Then he brought water to his grandmother. "Why," said grandmother, "My son, who are you? What are you?" "I am Falling Star," he answered, "I have killed the great thing that has been starving you for water."

Fall came. The boy started for another camp grandmother had told him about. Again he entered the lodge of an old woman sitting with her head hanging down and only one stick of wood. "Grandmother," he said, "I am very cold. Why don't you have a larger fire?"

"Oh, grandson," she said, "we cannot get any wood. There is a great *ve'kesehemestaa'e* (ghost bird, owl), who kills those who go for wood and puts them in its ear."

"Give me your rope and axe, and I will get some wood," said Falling Star. In the timber he had just finished tying a bundle of wood when the great owl appeared, took the boy and put him in its ear. With the arrows and bow the meadowlark had made for him, the boy shot an arrow into the brain of the owl and it fell down dead.

Creeping out of the ear, he carried the wood to his grandmother's lodge. "Now, grandmother, we will have a big fire and get warm." The grandmother told how the ghost bird was killed and it was announced through all the camp that Falling Star had killed the great owl that lived in the timber.

The snows came and Falling Star moved on to another camp of his people. Entering an old woman's lodge, he sat down. The old woman did not set food before him, so after some time he said to her, "Grandmother, I am hungry." "Oh, my son," she said, "We have no food; we cannot get any buffalo. A great white crow, *Okohke Ohvo'omaestse*, comes and drives them away."

"That is bad, very bad," Falling Star said, "I will see what I can do. Get me an old worn-out buffalo robe and ask the chief for two of the swiftest runners in the camp." Falling Star instructed the runners that when the buffalo came near he would be in a certain place, and when they ran away he would follow them. These young runners must come after him. When they overtook him they must shoot him and kill him and cut him open and leave him lying there.

Not long afterward the buffalo were near. White Crow called out, "They are coming! They are after you! Run! Run!" The buffalo ran, followed by an old scabby bull with little hair on his body that could not keep up with the herd. The two swift runners chased this bull and did not give up. At last they caught up with it, killed it, cut it open and left.

Looking back, they saw all kinds of birds, wolves and coyotes gathering about the carcass. White Crow flew over, landed nearby and said, "I wonder if this is Falling Star?" It kept getting closer and said, "Leave the eyes for me; do not touch the eyes. I wonder if this is Falling Star?" Just as it was about to peck the eyes, Falling Star reached out and caught it by the legs. All the birds flew away, and the coyotes and wolves scattered.

Falling Star brought White Crow to his grandmother's lodge and sent for one of the soldier bands and the chief to decide what to do with it. The chief said, "I will take it to my lodge and tie it in the smokehole and smoke it to death." But White Crow escaped. It was miraculously recaptured and put to death. After this the people caught many buffalo and said, "Now we are saved! Now we can have plenty to eat."

Next Falling Star struggles against *Vo'keme* (Old Man Winter). He attempts to destroy Old Man and his family, but one child escapes, so there continues to be snow. At the next camp he takes on Double Eyes, who has bitten off people's ears to make a necklace for himself. Following Falling Star's instructions the people trap Double Eyes in a lodge, throw grease on the fire, and shake a medicine rattle until he falls down dead. The people retrieve their ears, and Falling Star prepares a sweat lodge in which their ears are healed.

At the last camp, it is the old woman he meets in the lodge who is herself wounding the people by scalping them so she can use the scalps to decorate her robe. He outwits and kills her. The people recognize their scalps, and Falling Star heals the scalps on their heads in a sweat lodge. It was in this camp that a lodge had been built for him and a girl was waiting to marry him. Falling Star married the girl and "lived always with these people."

I had to think long and hard after reading this old Cheyenne story. It acknowledges that wounds are not always caused by supernatural powers beyond the people's control. Double Eyes, the medicine man, and the old woman we might name Scalp Snatcher violate the security and peace of the camp from within, just as the "Soul Snatcher" violated our daughter from within a circle we presumed safe.

Was it also possible that this strange myth of the son of the star father and the human mother, who comes from above to minister to the people's helplessness, who overcomes their enemies without and within, who dies and yet is alive, who heals their wounds, may actually foreshadow the even stranger story in which the Creator of all came among us in the person of Jesus, Immanuel, God with us?

I remember reading that Don Richardson, a missionary to the Sawi people of Irian Jaya, found it impossible to convey the story of the Creator's coming to earth in a way that made sense to the Sawi until he observed the making of a peace pact between two hostile groups. Each side exchanged one of their children for a child from the enemy side. So long as this "Peace Child" prospered, peace was preserved. Only when the Sawi began to understand Jesus as the "Peace Child," a child who came to restore the relationship between them and their Creator, did the message begin to change lives.[26]

More subtly, the Falling Star myth gives us but a hint of the One who "took up our infirmities and carried our sorrows...by [whose] wounds we are healed" (Isaiah 53: 4,5). Yet it is not, I think, an accident that the hint is there. Richardson is convinced that in the culture and stories of most of earth's peoples there are what he calls "redemptive analogies"—metaphors, pictures and stepping stones that point to what God is doing, has done, and will do, in that society through Jesus Christ.[27] I believe that the Falling Star story is such a stepping stone.

Chapter 23

There Is Another Funeral

There is another funeral.
I see them carrying the box.

I was at the funeral.
I didn't know who had died.

Mother played the piano.
Daddy gave the sermon.
We didn't have weddings much.

Every shovel of dirt
went heavy into the hole,
thud, thud, thud.

The women wailing,
blood dripping from wrists,
and the men shoveling.

The last shovelful
closed the cycle of things.

Now they have green stuff
and a gaping hole—
the casket sitting there.

There is no last shovelful
to cry into and no filled hole.

▂ Burying My Mother

We were standing in the tree-shaded cemetery north of the almost-extinct town of Zimmerdale, Kansas. We had just recently moved from our home among the Cheyenne in Montana to Newton, Kansas, where I was to work out of the Commission on Home Ministries' mission office. My mother had been moved from a care facility in Mountain Lake, Minnesota, to the Bethel Home in Newton, and my father joined us in our newly-purchased home.

Now, only 12 months since our move and in the midst of some difficult cultural adjustments, we were burying my mother. The service was familiar, yet somehow strange. The pile of earth taken from the newly-opened grave had been carefully covered with plastic imitation grass. There was a tent to shelter some of the mourners from the August sun. Pastor Paul Isaac repeated the familiar words from John's gospel, "I am the resurrection and the life," saith the Lord, "he that believeth in me, though he were dead, yet shall he live." A prayer was uttered committing mother's body to rest and her spirit to the Lord.

At that point it became clear that the funeral was over. People began talking to each other. The flower-covered casket still hung in its chrome-plated frame over the waiting hole in the earth. Words of caring and sympathy were given to us, but our five daughters looked at us in bewilderment. "Aren't we going to bury grandma?" they finally asked.

Then we remembered that the only funerals they had seen were Cheyenne funerals, and Cheyenne funerals did not end like this. After the service in the church at Busby the body would have been taken in a wagon or pickup truck (or nowadays in a hearse) to the fenced-off plot of prairie grass on the slope of the hill overlooking the community. Those who had been in the church service would be joined by other men, women and children from the village on the way to the graveyard.

After Cheyenne songs, the pastor's prayer and words of committal, everyone would have been given the opportunity to take a last look, to touch a cheek or motionless hand as tearful farewells were said. High-pitched wailing, different from other crying, expressed grief over the death. Occasionally women would cut short their long black hair or slash their arms or legs and let them bleed to dramatize the pain and finality of their loss. Then the men would lower the wooden box into the grave, using ropes or the straps that the pastor kept for that purpose.

I remembered a funeral early in our stay at Busby for the crippled son of *Voo'kooma* (White Blanket). After others had said their farewells, White Blanket, who we knew as Davis Bailey, had some things he wanted to place in the grave. The spirit of his son was on a journey to the camp of the dead, and might need some things: crutches, a suitcase of clothing, a few treasured articles, and a bit of food.

Typical Cheyenne burial.   *(JOHN BOEHR PHOTO)*

With these things placed beside the box, some of the men drove their shovels into the sandy brown heap of earth and began to fill the grave.

Children were always present at funerals, taking in all that was happening, looking down into the filling grave, listening to the sounds, watching the faces of the people. When the grave was full and the heap of earth covering it smoothly shaped, people placed flowers and wreaths, real and artificial, over the bare soil.

It had not always been that way. When the Cheyennes roamed the plains in the Time of the Buffalo, a body might be wrapped in a robe and placed in a tree, on a scaffold, in a crevice in the rocks, left in a tipi, or simply laid on the prairie and covered with rocks. Later, in the early reservation days, the body might be placed in a wooden box and left on the side of a hill. Sometimes such "burials" were vandalized by thieves, who stole beadwork or other ornaments from the bodies.

But the Cheyenne funerals we participated in did not even end with the filling of the grave and the decoration of the fresh earth. People remained at the grave as the family and relatives of the one who had died honored their loved one by giving gifts. The camp crier would call out in a voice that could be heard over the entire village, saying something like this: "Walks on the Ground, come here. Three Fingers wants you to come and receive this gift and shake his hand since he will never see his friend Limpy again." The gift given in honor of the one who died might be a horse, a blanket, a shawl, money, a table covered with dishes, or other valuables.

Bear Sole told me that in the old days, if a man lost his wife, others would give away all his property to people he was not related to, and he would walk away from the burial with nothing. He had to start over again. After the death the tipi belonging to the one who had died would be destroyed. A log house might be abandoned or burned. Or, in later years, a house might not be lived in again for some months.

It should not have seemed strange to us that our children were disturbed when grandma's funeral suddenly stopped when it was only half finished.

Death was a frequent visitor among the Cheyenne. Once High Hawk was reading obituaries in *The Mennonite* magazine and commented to me, "God surely has been good to your people, look how long they live." The diseases brought to this continent by Europeans were still taking a heavy toll among the Cheyenne. When we arrived, tuberculosis was the most deadly, as measles had once been. Almost every year, a child or two died of pneumonia after the mid-winter dances that followed Christmas.

As soon as the Indian Health Service began to win the fight against tuberculosis, other diseases became major problems—gallstones, diabetes. Then alcoholism began to take its deadly harvest among the Cheyenne people. One day Spotted Antelope and I started to list all the people we could remember who had died as a result of alcohol abuse, or the fights and wrecks that often accompanied it. It did not take long to come up with 75 names, most of them from our small community of Busby with only some 500 people. There were many funerals.

Gradually, the customs of the white man began to leave their mark on Cheyenne funerals. It became more common to purchase a casket and use the services of undertakers. Undertakers who were sensitive to Cheyenne customs were much appreciated. But the Cheyenne community became more subdued in its public mourning. Had they noticed how we whites hesitated to cry or show grief in public? But some customs do persist: A recent funeral I attended the family buried provisions for the trail to the land of the dead along with their loved one's body.

I was concerned to notice that public drinking sometimes seemed to have taken the place of public mourning. I remember how troubled I was at the funeral of a youth whose death was directly caused by alcohol to discover that his entire family was intoxicated. Alcohol's trail does not end at the grave. The memories of physical, emotional and sexual abuse, often triggered by abuse of alcohol, may leave footprints of loneliness, fear, and self-hate in the paths of those who walk away from the grave, having said farewell. It is as if death were reaching for their lives, too.

How much better when mourning can be expressed, the grave covered, the gifts given, the emptiness filled with God's Spirit, and a fresh start in life initiated. How much more beautiful when instead of just mourning those who have passed away we can look forward in hope to the time when death itself will have passed away.

> Then I saw a new heaven and a new earth; for the first heaven and the first earth had passed away, and the sea was no more... And I heard a loud voice from the throne saying,
>
> > See, the home of God is among mortals.
> > He will dwell with them as their God;
> > They will be his peoples,
> >
> > and God himself will be with them;
> > he will wipe every tear from their eyes
> >
> > Death will be no more;
> > mourning and crying and pain will be no more,
> > for the first things have passed away.
> > *Revelation 21:1, 3-5*
> > *(New Revised Standard Version)*

Chapter 24

Loud Whiteness

"She got her diamond," they said.
I'd never seen any one get a diamond.
This loud whiteness is all around me.

When I'm here, I'm too brown
And when I'm there I'm too white.
Looking in from the outside.

The brownness is too quiet
and the whiteness is too loud.
I'm looking in from somewhere
not brown, not white.

▄ Culture and Christ

A Cheyenne man, a stranger to me, entered the home where we were gathered for a weeknight prayer meeting. No one got up. One of the group obviously recognized him and said quietly something like, "*Šaa, moneešeho'eho'ohtse*" (So, you've come to visit now?), followed by a rather formal handshake. No one introduced the stranger. I discovered later that he was the brother of the man in whose house we were meeting. They had not seen each other for some 40 years! It was only later as I reflected on the event that I realized how differently I might have welcomed a long-lost brother. But public expression of emotion at such a time would have seemed embarrassing, out of place, to a Cheyenne.

Once when we were taking a break from our ministry among the Cheyenne we spent a winter in Mountain Lake, Minnesota, serving part-time with Bethel Mennonite Church. A Cheyenne girl whom I will call Lorrie was living with us and attending school with our daughters. She developed a close friendship with our neighbor, grandmother Krause. Returning from a visit with her, Lorrie burst into the living room of our house, surprised me by giving me a hug, and excitedly told me of their conversation. With us she felt free to express the vivacious, exuberant side of her nature.

When spring came and our return to the Cheyenne people was near, Lorrie stopped in the middle of an animated conversation with our daughters, clapped her hand over her mouth and said, "I've got to stop this. It is only a month till we go home. My Cheyenne grandmother would not like this loud talk."

So if a Cheyenne marriage would not be anticipated by the giving of an expensive stone, or welcomed with excited exclamations and squeals of delight, how was it announced? I was told that in the Days of the Buffalo, a young Cheyenne man and woman who sat together at a tribal event sharing a blanket over their shoulders were letting everyone knew that they were married.

There was more to it than that, of course. The young man would
have given the parents of the bride horses to prove his skill, ability
and bravery. The relatives on one side of the marriage would have
invited those on the other to a feast at which gifts were given. Later the
guests at this feast would reciprocate by hosting a feast and giving gifts
to the relatives of the other side. In this way the relatives and the
community acknowledged the marriage and gave their approval.

But this Cheyenne way of recognizing a marriage did not fit with
the white man's rules. In the eyes of the government this was not yet
a marriage. So the Bureau of Indian Affairs officials put pressure on
couples to get "legally married," or as the Cheyenne saw it "to buy a
paper" (a marriage license). For non-Christians this must have been
especially awkward because the only obvious way to complete the
process was to go to a Christian pastor to be "married."

One couple—I'll call them *Homa'ke* (Little Beaver) and *Heove'e*
(Yellow Woman)—came and asked me to marry them. Actually they
already had lived in faithful union for decades and had raised their
children to maturity. Now they were responding to the pressure to get
legally married.

They were not Christians, and as far as I knew had no intention
of becoming Christians. My suggestion that a justice of the peace or
county judge could fill out the paper they had purchased and satisfy
the white man's law was not very helpful. The nearest judge was 50
miles away in Hardin, and the couple had no car. No one seemed to
know whether the Cheyenne tribal judge, 17 miles away, was author-
ized to perform marriages, or if a leader of the Peyote Eaters would
be an acceptable religious figure. The only reasonable option seemed
to be a Christian pastor or priest, so they had come to me.

I finally told them that if they were willing to make the same
promises to each other that Christians would be asked to make, I
would marry them. As I mailed the completed and properly wit-
nessed marriage certificate to the Big Horn County Courthouse I

wondered, and still do: should we Christian pastors, wary of too close a union between church and state, act as agents of the state in creating the formal legal documents that register marriages? My attempts to raise the possibility of legal recognition of traditional Cheyenne weddings did not accomplish much.

A Native American pastor of another tribe commented to me that he was so glad that a young couple from his congregation had had a Christian wedding rather than following tribal custom in getting married. "What makes a wedding 'Christian?'" I thought to myself. "Is the mutual washing of hair with yucca root soap and the symbolic entangling of the hair of the bride and groom, as was that tribe's custom, any less 'Christian' than the exchange of expensive jewelry? Did changing the symbols make the difference?" The question of whether the customs we were introducing were truly Christian or just the white man's way was deeply troubling. Now, many years later, I hear that Cheyenne Christians are using parts of customary Cheyenne ways in celebrating marriages. It seems good to me.

There were so many ways in which Cheyenne cultural values and those my wife and I had grown up with differed. I was helped a great deal early on by an Indian elder speaking at a National Fellowship of Indian Workers meeting in Colorado. He provided us with two lists of differing cultural values something like the following:

Generosity	Thrift
Patience	Action
Cooperation	Competition
Modesty	Self-confidence
Respect for Age	Stress on Youth
Live for Today	Plan for Tomorrow
Harmony with Nature	Mastery over Nature
The Old Ways are Best	The New Way is Best
Time is with Us	Time Flies

Community	Individuality
Non-Scientific	Scientific
Practical	Theoretical
Religion Permeates All of Life	Religion is a Segment of Life

As I pondered these lists I began to see more clearly that the values of one culture are not necessarily superior or inferior, better or worse, than those of another culture, but simply different. I saw myself reflected most often in the list on the right, and discovered that my Cheyenne friends were most often supporting the values listed on the left. For example, I considered myself a generous person, but I gradually realized that my thrift outshone my generosity, while the Cheyenne people were more generous than I dreamed of being.

Early in our life with the Cheyennes we had been pulled, perhaps somewhat unconsciously, into thinking that Cheyenne youth might be better off if they could live in a Christian home and attend school in one of the communities that Mennonites lived in. We helped arrange that, and found homes that would take students in. While this may have helped some youth adapt to the white man's ways, and showed them examples of Christian discipleship, it often created problems when they returned to their own community. They had missed out on some of the ways and the history of their own people. They were often left stranded between cultures, not really fitting in with either one.

Was it necessary or even helpful for Cheyennes to adopt white ways in order to become Christians? The early church struggled with a similar question. Should the non-Israelites who became Christians be required to become Jewish as the other early Christians were? Should they be circumcised? After much debate, the first church council credited the Holy Spirit with helping them to the decision that since God had accepted the Gentiles there was no need to require them to become Jewish (Acts 15). Nor should we insist that becoming "civilized" is necessary to becoming a Christian.

Chapter 25

Identity

I'm dying in a world without a face.
What's worth anything
in a world without a face?
I've seen you, heard, felt you,
but when you're gone
I can't remember your face.

When in my existence I know a face,
a face to remember,
then I will know that I am.

A Casket Called Despair

A new evangelist moved into Lame Deer, where we were then living, and parked his trailer near one of the Pentecostal churches. He talked of big plans for cooperative work among the churches, starting with an all-community summer Bible School for children. Ann was intrigued and went to hear him speak. She reported that he was an interesting speaker and had told some amazing stories of his conversion and experiences. "But," she said, "there is something that isn't quite right." It seemed more an intuition than a certainty, although she had seen some evidence of a lifestyle that did not quite fit with an evangelist to native people. "And why doesn't his wife wear a wedding band?" she added.

I didn't make too much of Ann's cautions because I thought a community Bible School was a good idea, and after all, I haven't worn my wedding ring either ever since it got caught in a tool and nearly took my finger off. I knew that a marriage commitment didn't depend on a ring.

So I continued discussions with the evangelist. He surprised me one day by talking about "our class" at The Bible Institute of Los Angeles (Biola), which I had attended for three years. He called other classmates by name and implied that I should remember him. I had no memory of him. He told me of his previous work of translating the New Testament into Apache. This caught my attention, because I happened to know the name of the woman affiliated with Wycliffe Bible Translators who was working on an Apache translation. I asked who would be publishing his translation. He named a respected Bible publishing house.

I was beginning to reconsider Ann's intuition. In response to my inquiry, a letter from Biola stated they had no student by his name on record. The publishing house said they published Bibles only in English. I felt I must confront the evangelist. I went to Busby where he had now parked his trailer only to find that he and his wife had hitched it up and left town the night before, leaving no inkling of their destination.

Later we learned that he had identified himself as a missionary when requesting credit from businesses in Billings and had left large unpaid bills behind. "Missionary" quickly become a bad name in Billings. The manager of our local trading post had been more cautious. He had asked for credit references. When he was given references to businesses in the Caribbean he decided not to extend credit. He and Ann had been much more perceptive than I.

We remember our Ann as a sturdy, happy, blond child with blue eyes and a bubbly laugh. As she grew she became a happy helper in the home, with a strong body and a positive spirit. In her teen years she managed the home when her mother was sick and her father busy. She was sensitive to the feelings and struggles of others. Even the plots of early Christian movies that we occasionally showed in church were almost more than she could watch. She preferred to stay home rather than cry in public. Television was not a problem; we had none.

Esther had grown up in a strict home and had high standards for her daughters. (She later realized that she wanted the behavior of her girls to prove that she was an adequate mother.) Grandmother Boehr (Esther's mother) had sent lovely dresses for Ann and her sister. In one of the after-church scuffles among the children, Ann ran into a fence rail and ripped her dress from waist to hem. Esther found her on her bed, crying, expecting punishment. Ann was consoled only when assured that

"I made it." Ann graduates from college.

the gathered skirt could be mended, and that no one would be able
to tell that it had been torn.

Ann had an eye for beauty, in nature and in personal grooming.
A slight learning hindrance that caused her to mix the order of let-
ters in spelling and to have some difficulty in math created some
frustration at school, yet she was the first of our five daughters to
graduate from college. She showed wisdom beyond her years in in-
tuitive thinking. How little we knew of the ongoing struggle and
storm in her life. That she was also conscious of the storms in the
lives of the people with whom we lived is indicated in her poem:

> Your eyes are boiling,
>> yet you're listless like stagnant water.
> Bitterness heats your soul to liquid rock,
>> but your lukewarm speech says nothing.
> The lines of your face are a passionless pallor,
>> and you lie in this casket called despair.
> Anger murdered your life but you don't even feel it.

Though we were unaware of Ann's eroding sense of identity, the
evidence of a similar loss among the Cheyenne people was all around
us. Forced to deny their language, to speak a foreign tongue, to use
names bestowed by the intruders, to have decisions that affected
their lives made without consultation, restricted to an area where
there were not enough resources for traditional hunting nor, it seemed,
for the farming that the white man tried to introduce, even some
Cheyennes told their children: "You can't make it, you're just an
Indian."

This chipping away at Cheyenne identity was often subtle. When
we arrived on the reservation we were addressed as "Mr. and Mrs.
Wenger," as were all white people. Cheyenne people, on the other
hand, were usually addressed by their first names—their English

names, that is. Their real Cheyenne names were difficult for whites to pronounce, and early record keepers apparently simply supplied some people with English first names. The Cheyenne, like the patriarchs of the Old Testament, had not felt it necessary to use family names, but how could whites keep records without them? So the record keepers asked for translations of the father's name, which thereafter was designated the family name.

Thus *Voestaeso* (Little White Male Buffalo Calf) became "Willie." A translation of his father's name, *Eše'he Ohme'ehnestse*, provided the family name, "Risingsun." *Soena'hane'e* (Kills Through the Enemy Woman) became "Maggie," and her husband's father's name *Nahkohno'kaestse* became the family name, "One Bear." Today Cheyenne families usually give their children both Cheyenne and English names.

We felt more at ease when we ourselves were given Cheyenne names, and had learned enough of the language that we could use Cheyenne names in speaking to elders. Rodolphe Petter, the early missionary and Swiss linguist, tried to translate the meaning of my Swiss family name, "Wenger," into Cheyenne as *Vo'tanema'hahe* (Something shaped like a cheek; a friend). That still sounded foreign to Cheyenne ears, so I was often just called *Vo'tanotse* (Cheeks). Esther fared better, receiving a familiar Cheyenne name, *Voeše'e* (Happy Woman). When speaking English we continued to use the English first names of Cheyenne people and tried to make it clear that they should use our first names as well.

Beginning in 1904, the Bureau of Indian Affairs operated a school for the Cheyenne at Busby, then known as the Tongue River Boarding School. At one time in its history, no doubt for obscure reasons of administrative efficiency, menus for the meals at this, and probably many other Indian schools, were prepared somewhere in the Southwest—in Albuquerque, New Mexico, as I recall. The menus used a lot of beans, which may have been great for the tribes of the Southwest, but many Cheyenne children hated them. So the Cheyenne cooks had to throw the beans out. There seemed to be no way that they could change the system so they could cook foods that the school children liked.

In fact there was very little about the school that local people had any say about. Decisions were always made elsewhere. The local staff reported to someone in a distant city rather than to the community. No one on the staff spoke Cheyenne, except for some local people who drove buses, cooked, mined coal, tended furnaces, and the like. Teachers, with a few exceptions, often spent their weekends elsewhere, and never really got to know the parents of the children they were teaching.

High Hawk and others worked hard to get the school under the control of the Cheyenne tribal council, and finally succeeded. This and other similar actions began the task of giving back a face to the Cheyenne people.

Even with the best intentions, we missionaries often did things that also chipped away at Cheyenne identity. We, too, reported to a distant board. We failed to make a clear distinction between our role as church planters and that of Cheyenne leaders in the local church.

Busby school.

We made too many of the decisions, and were slow to give opportunity for local responsibility and accountability. The church retained a white face. Only when Cheyennes look at the Christian church and see a Cheyenne face will it be most effective in its task.

Words that the Creator once spoke to ancient Israel assuring them of their identity may now through Jesus be claimed by people from "every nation, tribe, people, and language" who follow him.

> Fear not, for I have redeemed you;
>> I have summoned you by name;
>> you are mine...
> For I am the LORD, your God,
>> the Holy One of Israel, your Savior;...
> Since you are precious and honored in my sight,
>> and because I love you.
> Do not be afraid, for I am with you;
>> I will bring your children from the east
>> and gather you from the west.
> I will say to the north, "Give them up!"
>> and to the south, "Do not hold them back."
> Bring my sons from afar
>> and my daughters from the ends of the earth—
>> everyone who is called by my name,
>> whom I created for my glory,
>> whom I formed and made.
> *Isaiah 43:1,3-7.*

Chapter 26

If You Weren't a Man

If you weren't a man.
I could receive you as lover.
I could be saved,

If you were still God
and had never come here
as a man.

If you weren't a man
I would believe You
to be the Christ.

How can you be the Christ
and be a man?

Ann and the Cheyenne People

A friend who works in the mental health field once told us, "The thing that does the most long-term damage to a woman is the violation of her body." She went on to say that this does not always mean rape. It might be other forms of violence.

In many ways we were thrilled to see our daughter Ann maturing and contributing. She completed two years of Bible School and three years of college, graduating with a degree in social work. Between school terms she volunteered to teach summer Bible school to Hopi children at Bacavi, Arizona, and worked with a mission at Logan, Utah. She gave leadership to young volunteers caring for severely retarded children at Wheatridge, Colorado. We were glad for her willingness to serve God and others.

With her older sister, Elizabeth, she took in an Inter-Varsity Christian Fellowship missions conference at Urbana, Illinois. She helped out with a one-week day camp for children in Liberal, Kansas. Temporary work in Bethel Home for the Aged enabled her to be near her grandmother, a resident there. After graduation from college she accepted a long-term volunteer assignment in Toronto, Canada, working with troubled teenage girls. She was with her older sister in Mexico City and Tlaxiaco, Oaxaca for four months helping before and after the birth of her niece.

Yet in spite of her sensitivity, caring, courage and leadership, there was a perplexing shadow over Ann's life. Could it have come from the rebellion and turmoil of the 1960s that she encountered in college? Why was she tense and ill at ease around men? With such obvious gifts, why did she lack self-esteem? Had losing three grandparents in eight months been too much?

Even more troubling were the hints that she was struggling to hold on to her faith in God. Most worrisome was her comment that she had thought of suicide. What was happening in our family? We thought we had been caring for our children., but there seemed to be nothing that we could say to restore Ann's trust and confidence and zest for life.

Although years had passed since the events described earlier in "The Dark One Comes," Ann had still not confided in us. She later described those damaging events in these words:

> There is a space for the holy.
> There is a place—full and silent.
> Invitation builds its center;
> Welcome calls out the sacred light.
>
> But you bulldozed the doors;
> You took the holy of holies.
> It is a place made only by invitation.
> You stole the treasure.

Had she talked with us about this experience of sexual assault earlier, would we have been able to hear her and help her? Would we have been able to understand that those few moments of violence would leave their mark on all her days? I doubt it. I had not yet learned how deep the spiritual and psychological damage could be when a woman's body is violated, her treasure stolen.

As I now think of those violent events of the past that for many years shadowed my daughter's relationship with God, I see parallels to that other violence that began 500 years ago when Europeans invaded the Americas.

Columbus was an enigmatic adventurer, openly referring to himself and his crew as Christians, and committed, as he told his sponsors Ferdinand and Isabella, to learn as much as he could of the peoples he expected to find and of the "measures which could be taken for their conversion to our Holy Faith." His very name, Christopher, means "Christ Bearer."[28]

Columbus was impressed with the inhabitants of the Indies. He wrote in his log, "They were well-built, with good bodies and handsome features....They do not bear arms and do not know them....[W]ith fifty men we could subjugate them all and make them do whatever we want." He was astounded by their generosity. "When you ask for something they have they never say no. To the contrary they offer to share with anyone."[29] The Spanish called these Arawak people, Tainos, meaning "noble" or "good."

Later, when it became clear that he could not load his ships with gold as he had promised, Columbus became desperate to show some kind of profit from his "enterprise." So he rounded up 1,500 Tainos and selected 500 to be sent to Spain to be sold as slaves. Two hundred died en route. Trying to get the gold that could be found only in tiny amounts in what is now Haiti, he required every Indian to bring in a certain amount of gold every three months. Those that failed had their hands cut off. "In two years, through murder, mutilation, or suicide, half of the 250,000 Indians on Haiti were dead." By 1650 none of the original Arawaks or their descendants were left on the island.[30] No doubt the new diseases that Europeans brought with them also contributed to the deaths. And perhaps only one Arawak, who had been taken to Spain and who died soon afterward, was converted to the "holy faith" by Columbus or his men.

Columbus initiated a pattern of confronting the native peoples with prideful conquest rather than sharing, listening and learning. Five hundred years later, his influence is still with us. The nature of the Creator as revealed to us in Jesus Christ has been so terribly distorted by the actions of some who claim to be his followers that many aboriginal people want nothing to do with the "white man's God."

One powerful clue to the differences between these cultures that clashed so tragically is the nature of leadership in each. I came to understand that the role of a chief among the plains Indians, for example, was quite different from the conception of leadership my own culture led me to expect. Esther and I once attended the installation of Arthur Sutton, a chief of the Arapaho tribe, as pastor of Zion Arapaho Mennonite Church in Canton, Oklahoma. The celebration ended with a feast, but Arthur was not eating. I urged him to join the line of people heaping their plates with food. After all, this was his occasion. I can still hear his quiet remark, "Chiefs always eat last."

Our friend *He'amavehonevestse* (Sky Chief), whom we usually called by his English name, Lawrence Hart, had told me of the training he received to be a chief among the Cheyennes, and this helped me to understand what Arthur meant. A chief was to be an example of humility and service to his people. If he, riding the trail, met someone afoot, he was expected to offer that person his horse. As leader of his people, he saw to it that everyone had food before he ate.

These and other instructions on the role of the chief came from *Motse'eoeve* (Sweet Medicine), the culture hero of the past whose teachings still guide the Cheyenne tribe. "You chiefs are peacemakers," he said. "Though your son might be killed in front of your tepee, you should take a peace pipe and smoke....If strangers come, you are the ones to give presents to them and invitations. When you meet someone or he comes to your tepee asking for anything, give it to him. Never refuse. Go outside your tepee and sing your chief's song, so all the people will know you have done something good."[31]

I once was told of an event in Birney that brought this admonition to life. One of the chiefs there was talking to a group of Cheyennes when a messenger arrived with the news that his son had been murdered. Yet the chief made no loud cries or threats of retaliation. He simply turned his back, walked away a few steps and sang his song.

Europeans, fresh from their experience with kings, assumed that each tribe had one chief who made decisions for the tribe and led them in battle. But the Cheyennes had a council of 44 chiefs, four of them head chiefs. Furthermore, although these men may once have been members of soldier societies that warred with other tribes, they now were peace chiefs. They were expected to lay aside their weapons and help to maintain peace within and without the tribe. Whites did not understand that the Cheyenne chief was essentially a man of peace.

Mo'ohtavetoo'o (Black Kettle) was such a peace chief. He had been a great warrior in his youth but during the turbulent years of 1860-1868 tried to keep peace between his people, the southern branch of the Cheyennes, and the whites. In 1863, he and Lean Bear were invited to visit the "Great Father," Abraham Lincoln, who gave them peace medals and papers certifying that they were good friends of the United States. Colonel Greenwood, Commissioner of Indian Affairs, gave Black Kettle a huge United States flag with white stars for the 34 states, and told him that as long as that flag flew above him no soldiers would ever fire upon him. Black Kettle was very proud of the flag and flew it over his tipi whenever in permanent camp.[32]

Back on the plains, though, soldiers shot and killed Lean Bear even as he attempted to approach them to show his medal and papers. A battle ensued, with Black Kettle trying to stop the fighting. Later he accompanied other Cheyenne and Arapaho chiefs to Denver to try to establish peace. The meeting was inconclusive, since Governor Evans had already asked all citizens to kill Indians on sight, and the Reverend John Milton Chivington, a former Methodist minister, now a colonel in charge of the Colorado Militia, was itching to get started.

Assured by the military at Fort Lyon that the Cheyennes would be safe at Black Kettle's winter camp at Sand Creek, the young men went out to hunt. At dawn on November 28, 1864, Colonel Chivington, supported by Major Anthony of Fort Lyon, attacked the Cheyenne camp. White Antelope went to meet the soldiers to show his peace medal, but was shot down. Black Kettle raised his US flag and a white flag over his tipi and stayed until most of the women and children had fled. As he tried to escape with his wife, she was hit by a bullet and appeared to be dead. Soldiers shot her eight more times while she lay there, but miraculously she survived. Black Kettle later rescued her.[33]

In spite of the betrayal at Sand Creek and rejection by many of his own people, especially the Dog Soldiers, Black Kettle made yet another attempt at peace with the white man by participating in the talks on Medicine Lodge Creek. He agreed to be settled on a reservation south of the Arkansas River. In the meantime, he established his village on the Washita. Hearing rumors of soldiers coming, he traveled 100 miles to Fort Cobb to ask permission to move there for protection. Fort Commander General William B. Hazen refused, knowing that General Sheridan planned a winter war against the Indians. He assured Black Kettle that his village would be safe on the Washita. Black Kettle returned and called a late-night council, but at dawn General Custer attacked the village and killed Black Kettle, his wife, and 101 others. Only 11 of the dead were warriors.[34]

Malcolm Wenger ponders Sand Creek massacre, 1990.

One cool fall day Esther and I visited the site of Black Kettle's Sand Creek tragedy on the high plains of eastern Colorado. We passed through the town named in honor of Colonel Chivington, now only a few abandoned buildings and a sign along a railroad track. One wall bore a fading portrait of Black Kettle.

Further on in an emptiness of grass with a few leafless tree skeletons standing by the dry wash of Sand Creek was the place where Black Kettle's camp once stood and where the relatives of people we know suffered and died. It would not seem strange to us if the survivors and their descendants would say of the Christ, "If you weren't a white man, we could be saved." Only by a gracious miracle of the Spirit of God are some Cheyennes willing to forgive and become brothers and sisters with white people in the Christian family.

Terry Widrick, a Mohawk friend from Manitoba, suggests that, "the Native people, like the Hebrews of the Old Testament, are waiting for the true Christ to come." For him the Christ identified with the Columbus conquest, land takeover, oppression and power is a violent Christ, not the healing, serving Jesus of the New Testament.[35]

We white Christians would do well to join the prophet Daniel in his prayer of confession:

> O Lord, the great and awesome God,
>> who keeps his covenant of love
>> with all who love him and obey his commands,
>> we have sinned and done wrong.
> We have been wicked and rebelled;
>> we have turned away from your commands and laws.
> We have not listened to your servants the prophets,
>> who spoke in your name to our kings,
>> our princes and our fathers,
>> and to all the people of the land....
>
> O Lord listen!
> O Lord forgive!
> O Lord hear and act!
> For your sake, O my God, do not delay,
> Because your city and your people bear your Name.
> *Daniel 9:4-7,19.*

Chapter 27

Gerry

I can smell the Pine-Sol
as if it were today
in that two-room cabin
with a batch of kids.

I knew you
from the first day
my sister had a
best friend.

Betsy and Gerry
playing dolls, sleeping over,
jumping across rooftops,
making mud pies.

So much gone by now,
too much pain,
too much booze,
in a place where pines
stand tall with dignity.

This rub
keeps grinding up my soul.
This wound
that doesn't go away.

But you went today—
you,
44,
gone.

▄ "Alcoholism Is a Terminal Illness"

Late in our years of ministry we were taking classes to learn more about the implacable foe that had done so much damage in the communities in which we lived, and one statement got my attention: "Alcoholism is a terminal illness." Was stopping the damage just a matter of willpower, or was alcoholism really a sickness unto death?

So many did die. Some with startling suddenness in the tearing crash of an out-of-control automobile (or did the hopelessness of the battle lead some to deliberately turn the car into the path of an oncoming truck?). A few died by a violent knife thrust or even the deadly shock of a bullet that sober heads might not have unleashed. For others death came painfully slowly as their liver atrophied, their brain cells diminished, and malnutrition set in after years in which alcohol's "empty calories" replaced healthy foods.

Arthur H., an Ojibwe elder who found hope after a long love affair with alcohol, says that addiction is an uncontrollable, over-

Fatal car wreck near "Jim Town."   *(TOEWS PHOTO, JULY 1963)*

powering force that becomes the most demanding thing in life. We saw firsthand that alcohol could become more powerful than the commitment to a job, the love of a mother for a child, the promise a husband gave to his wife, the desire to follow God—even the desire to stay alive. How painful it was to see our daughter's best friend gradually snared by this addiction.

Arthur H. tells how desperately he tried to avoid the losses that alcoholism brings. Still they came. As he landed in the drunk tank again and again, he lost his position as pastor, his self-esteem, his wife and four children to divorce, his health, his driver's license, his car, his qualities of character, and his moral and spiritual strength.

And he is one of the success stories. Through the help of a loved one, a knowledgeable counselor, a roller-coaster ride through treatment programs, Alcoholics Anonymous (AA) meetings, immersion in the Scriptures and helpful books, he finally achieved sobriety and got back on his feet spiritually. It took him 13 years.[36]

Recently we traveled to Manitoba to participate in Assembly, a gathering of Christians from Native churches among the Mennonites. Kills on the Water (Leonard Little Wolf), director of Pre-School and Head Start for the Northern Cheyennes, told his story to the hundred or so people gathered in the Hollow Water School. "I am a walking miracle," he told us. He said that he had spent 13 years drinking and now for 17 years had been a "recovering alcoholic."

He told of wrecked cars and motorcycles, of "blackouts" and "D.T.'s" (the violent restlessness and terrifying hallucinations of alcohol withdrawal known as delirium tremens). He would sometimes wake up in the morning with no idea of what had happened the night before, and anxiously go out to check his car to see if it was damaged or if someone was sleeping in the back seat. He also remembered "throwing my wife and kid out of the house."

Through an "intervention" arranged by his wife, caring friends and the pastor, he began to see his need and was willing to get help. He now meets regularly with the AA group in his church. "Miracles do happen," he said. "Now I count my blessings. I let go and let God." He concluded by reading the Apostle Paul's words to the Ephesian church:

> Finally let the mighty strength of the Lord make you strong.
> Put on all the armor God gives,
> so you can defend yourself against the devil's tricks.
> We are not fighting against humans.
> We are fighting against forces and authorities
> and against rulers of darkness and powers in the spiritual world.
> So put on all the armor that God gives.
> Then when that evil day comes, you will be able to defend yourself.
> And when the battle is over, you will still be standing firm....
> Never stop praying....
> Ephesians 6:10-13,18 (Contemporary English Version)

When our daughter's friend Gerry realized that *Naevehane*, the grim reaper, was waiting for her, she called her children to her bedside to tell them, "I'm sorry, I'm so sorry."

Ann visits at Gerry's home.

> My soul thirsts for God,
>   for the living God.
> When shall I come and behold
>   the face of God?
> My tears have been my food
>   day and night.
> While people say to me continually,
>   "Where is your God?"
> *Psalm 42:2-3. (New Revised Standard Version)*

Chapter 28

An Angel

The night is light and wispy,
Opposing itself to my steaming and cluttered thoughts.
Sleep is longing to come and cover this war.
It is trapped just outside this strife and self-incrimination.

Can a person from the past so infest the aura of a dark room?
Finally sleep—courageous, though less than settled.

At three a.m. a presence penetrates.
The room is cleaned, swept of its suffering, its scathing insanity.
An angel has come, it's sure, and set all at rest.

I know I felt a sitting on the bed,
A cleanness that hitherto was sorely missed,
And I am blessed.

▅ Pastor Little Bear Meets an Angel

"What do you think about angels, their role and ministry? There is so much talk about angels nowadays among white Christians; what is an Indian Christian point of view?"

The questions came from Martin Cross, a Metis from Saskatchewan, and were directed to a panel on "Christ and Culture" at a Native Assembly meeting in Manitoba. The panel members, Steve Cheramie Risingsun of Louisiana, Henry Neufeld of Manitoba, Little Bear (Joe Walks Along) of Montana, Marvin Yoyokie of Arizona and Iris Hartshorn of Pennsylvania, usually looked at each other first to see who was most ready to venture an answer. But this time Joe Walks Along spoke up immediately. "I would like to speak to that question," he said, raising his index finger.

Joe stood to emphasize his words. "Angels are God's helpers," he began, "and I have had some experience with that. Many years ago my wife and family and I were invited to speak at the Arvada Mennonite Church near Denver, Colorado. After a long day driving the 500 or so miles from Lame Deer we were approaching the edge of Denver when I suddenly realized I had not brought along the address of the church nor did I have a phone number to call.

"What are we going to do?" I asked my wife Victoria. "There must be about two million people living around here and it's almost midnight. This is not going to be like finding a place in Lame Deer."

"Maybe we should just turn around and go home," she replied. We were too tired to drive all night so I said, "I'll just turn off at the next exit and see what we can find." As we drove slowly up a side street we came to a high building with glass sides. It must have been some kind of a business building. Then I noticed a man standing in front of it.

I told Victoria, "I'll just park here and go over and talk to that man." He was dressed in a dark suit and was wearing a tie. He looked like a businessman. I told him about the meeting we were going to and that we did not know where the church was located. I don't remember that I told him my name.

The man told me, "Just go right on down this street to the second stop light. You will be shown where to go." So we went. At the stoplight a car drove up alongside and someone asked: "Are you Joe Walks Along?" "Yes," I said. "Follow me," he said, and drove off.

We drove a long way, maybe 20 miles. He led us into a cul-de-sac, to a church building, waved at us and drove off. I never did get a good look at him, but that was the place that we were looking for.

Later Joe learned that the church had been having a party that evening honoring volunteer workers and had its phone off the hook. Even if he had had a telephone number he would not have been able to get directions to the church.

"I believe God sends his helpers, his angels," Joe concluded.

> What are the angels, then?
> They are spirits who serve God
> and are sent by him
> to help those who are to receive salvation.
> *Hebrews 1:14 (Today's English Version)*

Chapter 29

A Tribute to a Priest of Shalom

He sat with me through empty places,
making them full in yielded listening
and endless hoping.

My tears he held in shameless large hands,
helping my heart up out of its dying,
cloaking its naked shivering in tenderness.

He mediated the flight
of the ominous bird at my shoulder,
Then prayed into the barrenness
left on the ground of my soul.

When love astonished my heart,
we drank the warmth of the holy light,
shimmered in its gentle blowing
and danced in delight.

The brothers and sisters,
the Master, the Majesty, the Holy Wind,
the Priest of Shalom and I.

◣ Healing Begins

We felt so helpless! But when we did not know how to come to the aid of our troubled daughter, again and again, the "Priest of Shalom" was there.

A young couple in Newton, Kansas, perhaps going through some of their own questioning, opened their home and their lives to struggling young adults, or as Ann put it, they "took in lost Mennonite young people." Here she found acceptance, fellowship, and a listening ear.

Another group of young people seeking a fresh reality in their Christian walk formed a church in which they shared their money as well as fellowship and lived together in households, seeking to be more accountable to one another and to God. The hope they offered attracted our daughter and other struggling persons. Sometimes while "resting in the Spirit" they would surround a troubled one with quiet waiting, listening and prayer, asking what the person was feeling and where the tears were coming from and perhaps giving a word of insight or comfort from the Lord. In the arms of this caring and nurturing community, New Creation Fellowship, Ann was able to reclaim memories of her past and begin to share them with others. We thought we saw healing beginning.

Ann had good male friends, people she could talk to, but none of these relationships led in the direction of marriage. As she later told us, "My image of maleness, my male trust, had been damaged." In the pain of loss and disappointment, she decided, "I have to leave, I am not sure why but I have to leave." So she moved to Indiana to start afresh in a new community.

Her only uncle, Orlando Schmidt, helped her, but with little money it was a hard struggle to find work, housing, and new friends. In her first apartment she was neighbor to drug users on one side and loud quarreling on another. "Am I going to get raped or beat up?" she

Esther visiting at Ann's apartment.

wondered. "I would wake up at night and pray. There was nothing I could do but pray. Somebody helped me. It was dangerous."

When many of my responsibilities to Native American churches had been taken over by the Mennonite Indian Leader's Council, it seemed best to give them freedom to work without me looking over their shoulder. I accepted an invitation to pastor a Metis (mixed ancestry) church in Canada. Though small, the congregation was very diverse. When one of the youths in the congregation painted Christmas greetings on the front window of the church, he wanted to use all the languages spoken or understood by people in the congregation, and came up with English, German, Polish, Icelandic, Ukrainian, Cree and Saulteaux.

Still confronted with problems of alcohol abuse in our new community, Esther and I took a week of alcoholism training sponsored by the province of Manitoba that taught us something about addictions, those frail crutches for the brokenness of life. Even with our new understandings I was unable to help the husband of a Christian sister to throw away his crutch. But the understandings did help when Ann told us that she realized she was using food—a package of sweet rolls at a sitting—to deal with some of the pains in her life. We could encourage and support her in her choice to attend Al-Anon meetings.

In an attempt to be more helpful to people in our congregation that were having struggles in their marriages we responded to an invitation to participate in a Marriage Encounter weekend. During these intense Friday-night-to-Sunday-night sessions in a motel (with TV off limits) we heard the stories of other couples and realized that there were issues we needed to deal with in our own relationship. I was able to share with Esther my feeling of being "managed" when she kept reminding me of things I should be doing. It also became clear to me that there were better ways of dealing with conflict and anger than my choice of going into a depression that could make me useless for hours at a time. We were encouraged to take time to communicate with each other, sharing feelings and concerns. We began to understand that we were, as Henri Nouwen put it, "wounded healers."[37] At the closing session we were surprised to meet a couple, strangers to us, who had been praying for us all weekend.

Ann's later journey included a Christian fellowship that was helpful initially, but later marred by dissension. Silent retreats at a convent became times of healing. Talking things over with a counselor was often profitable but expensive. Health struggles complicated matters. Ann read widely and sometimes sent us books or copies of articles that she had found helpful. As I write, I remember one that she gave me that I never finished reading. My interests obviously were still elsewhere.

Home for Christmas one year she brought along some of the poems included in this book and read them to the family. This gave us new insight into her struggles. Later, perhaps sensing that we were more ready to hear, and with the encouragement of her counselor, she told us about the attempted rapes that had happened some 14 years earlier.

Newly sensitized, we noticed a workshop on sexual abuse at a triennial Mennonite conference led by a Christian woman counselor. Esther attended and was shocked to learn how frequently abuse of family members happened within the church. Later we had the privilege of being "friendly visitors" to many congregations and were again surprised to hear how often stories of abuse came up in conversations. Esther introduced to women's groups the newly published "Purple Packet" prepared by the Mennonite Central Committee to raise awareness of this problem and what might be done when it occurred.

Ann's counselor challenged her to write a letter to the perpetrator. When she finished, the counselor said, "Now read it to me." Ann discovered that it was still too painful to read the letter aloud. But later she got up the courage to send it to leaders in the Cheyenne churches and asked if they would read the letter to him. "No more secrets," she said. "Perhaps making this known will protect someone else."

Then some native friends invited Esther and me to a Thanksgiving feast. To our dismay, we learned that although the young man who had assaulted Ann lived far away, he too would be a guest at the feast. I and another of our daughters asked if we could meet him before the feast. He was now in training to be a Christian evangelist. When we confronted him with the past, he admitted it, but passed it off as teenage lust that should have been forgiven and forgotten. We read a copy of Ann's letter to him and offered to pass on to her any response he might want to make (she was still anxious about letting him know where she lived). He chose not to respond.

During a visit with Ann we asked if we might go with her to a session with her counselor. She seemed surprised that we would be willing to do this and thanked us afterward. Later that evening we were awed to feel the depth of her pain as she poured it out to us. We understood more clearly the losses that she, and we, have suffered as a result of that long-ago event.

The wounds of sexual abuse heal very slowly if at all. But, we were encouraged that exposing the secret and writing the letter seemed to have lifted much of the load from Ann. She is now part of a church that has taken in many hurting people, and she has a ministry to women with similar pain.

As wounded healers we have learned that there are times when we have no answers. These are times for prayer, for trust in God, for standing back and watching God at work. There was a young couple attending our church in Manitoba whom we'll call Tom and Thelma. Tom had a good job and provided well for his wife and two beautiful children. Thelma was of Metis ancestry and met Tom while traveling in Europe. We were happy to have them in the congregation although Tom did not always attend with the rest of the family.

One of the deep scars in Tom's life, we learned, was the illness and death of his mother during his childhood in England. He wanted to be with her but was told to be quiet and not bother her though he could hear her cries of pain. He now understands that she was dying of incurable cancer. When he and Thelma wanted to get married, his father did not approve. They got married anyway, and moved to Canada, which left a deep gulf between him and his father.

It was around Christmas time one year that Tom told Thelma, "I have to leave. It's not that I have anything against you, but I just have to go." Thelma had noticed his restlessness but told us that she knew of nothing that would have driven him away. When he returned to pick up some of his clothing, his young son followed him out the door crying, "Daddy, Daddy," but he did not look back. He left no word as to where he was going.

Rumor had it that there was another woman and that the trouble was rooted in gatherings with friends to view pornographic movies. Thelma was forced to find work to support herself and her children. Child care while she was at work was a problem, although her younger brother helped out at times. We shifted the Wednesday night prayer meetings to her home so she could put her children to sleep and still participate. Those meetings became special times for us.

Some co-workers told her: "Your husband walked out on you." "Get even with him. Have an affair with someone else." "Lots of guys would take you out." But she refused. She believed God had made them a family and would bring them together again. She said nothing bad about her husband to her children.

At one of our gatherings she told us that she had taken a long drive on dark wintry roads while her brother was caring for the children. She had a vision of Tom's face, and of Jesus putting his gentle hand on her shoulder. Soon friends tipped her off that her husband was living in a distant city.

One evening she came with a friend to prayer meeting bubbling with excitement about a book they had found in a store. What caught their eye was the title, *Caring Enough Not to Forgive*. Intrigued, they scanned it and discovered that it was a double book. On the flip side was the second title, *Caring Enough to Forgive*. As they shared with us some of the insights of the author, David Augsburger, a lively discussion followed. We wondered if forgiveness was possible in situations such as she and her friend had experienced, and if so when and how it should happen.[38]

Months went by. God gave her another vision. This time she saw her husband sitting in a small room, alone and dejected. We joined her in prayer, asking if this was the time for her to travel to the distant city and contact him. She came to the conviction that the time was ripe and made the trip.

She did not immediately try to contact her husband, but waited until she was assured that it was the Lord's time. Then, through someone who knew them both, she made contact. She discovered that her husband had long wanted to come back to her but felt so badly about what he had done that he could not find the courage to get in touch. They settled in that city and went about the task of rebuilding their marriage. Thelma reached out to Tom's father, and a warm relationship developed.

> Trust in the LORD and do good;
>   live in the land and be safe.
> Seek your happiness in the LORD
>   and he will give you your heart's desire.

Give yourself to the LORD;
  trust in him, and he will help you;
he will make your righteousness shine
  like the noonday sun.

Be patient and wait for the LORD to act;
  don't be worried about those who prosper
  or those who succeed in their evil plans.
Psalm 37:3-7 (Today's English Version)

Chapter 30

You Have Come

YOU have come and caught me up
into your tenderness.

I have never been so loved before.

YOU, once so far off, have come
and twined my heart into Your love.

Red Medicine Woman Receives New Songs

You have come!

The old questions may still echo: Why was I "driven like a tumbleweed against the barbs of unknown fences?" "How can I be without you? Yet I am?" Why am I here "dying in a world without a face?" "Why are men in your image?"

But somehow the "whys" have lost their sting in the presence of Jesus, in the knowledge of being accepted by the Creator's beloved Son. How wonderful to hear our daughter express her assurance of being truly loved by the One who once seemed so far away.

Ma'seeota'e (Red Medicine Woman), known in English as Maude Fightingbear, was not a stranger to pain. All of her children died. Her marriage failed. In her autumn years she seemed alone except for young girls she took into her home. But through the word of God in the hands and lives of caring people, she had come to trust and love the Creator as the searching, merciful and forgiving God, the giver of grace, who had come looking for us in the person of Jesus. She learned that through his death and resurrection our pains and hurts could be healed, our sins forgiven. She choose to walk the Jesus road.

Hevovetaso Ohtameohtsestse (Whirlwind Walking), joined her on her journey. We usually called him William Fightingbear. Both Red Medicine Woman and Whirlwind Walking learned to read the scriptures well in Cheyenne and English and loved the

Red Medicine Woman and Whirlwind Walking. (Maude and William Fightingbear.)

Word. They became a close brother and sister in the faith. She gave
Cheyenne names to three of our daughters; he helped with the preach-
ing; she expressed her faith in song.

> The Lord gave me his son.
> He clothed me with the Victor.
> That's why I am happy.[39]

We learned something about prejudice when we took them with
us to Billings for medical appointments. The better hotels were full.
One that had a vacancy refused Whirlwind Walking and Red Medi-
cine Woman, but would have taken us. We offered to share a room
with them but the unyielding response was, "No, I can't rent to
Indians. I would lose other customers." He lost us. Frustrated, we
left and finally found rooms for all of us in a poorly-kept hotel.

When Red Medicine Woman got sick and depressed and the
doctors were puzzled, we made space for them in the log house next
door that had been our first home and now was partly used for Sun-
day School. It was winter and their home was about 15 miles from
town. Whirlwind Walking was not well either. Once during her weeks
of illness Red Medicine Woman asked for anointing in keeping with
James 5:13-20. After a church service some of the Christians came
to her bedside, put oil on her forehead, laid hands on her and prayed.
Gradually she got better.

Years later, Esther became very ill with hepatitis. People were
afraid of contracting it, so she had few visitors. It was Red Medicine
Woman and Whirlwind Walking who came to her upstairs bedroom
to pray for her healing.

When the psalmists and Isaiah urged their hearers to "sing to
the Lord a new song" I think of Red Medicine Woman, singer of new
songs to the Lord—songs that celebrated the new covenant the Crea-
tor had made with his people. She used melodies that she had learned

in her youth, or new ones given in answer to prayer. In either case they were shaped by the venerable tradition of Cheyenne music. The words reflected her knowledge of the Bible.

When Red Medicine Woman was asked about the inspiration for her songs she often told of the time her brother had disappeared. His car had been found abandoned and she feared he had been killed. She gave herself to much prayer, and to her joy, he was found alive. Then she said, "I told the Lord, I'm gonna praise you in song.... Here's the way I'm gonna sing it with words, and [you] give me the tune how it's going to go. I just kept on praying, maybe for four days I kept asking him. I didn't give up."

Not long afterward, as she and Whirlwind Walking were return-ing to their home on upper Rosebud Creek, their car stalled. Deep in thought about the song, she let her husband try to figure out the problem, while she prayed by some tall bushes nearby. "Then I tried to sing again," she said. "My, I really sang right, like something lifted me up, like I was really lifted up. My, I really got happy. That's how I got this song." Of another song she said, "That's just how it came to me...God must have directed me that way. The Holy Spirit teaches me that way, I think. That's what I believe."[40]

When High Hawk had helped the Northern Cheyenne Tribe gain control of the Busby schools formerly operated by the Bureau of Indian Affairs, one of the changes they decided on was to add a music teacher to the school staff. The man they choose to fill the position came to it in an unexpected and circuitous way.

Dave Graber, university graduate in music from Iowa, moved to Boise, Idaho, to help with a church planting venture. He and his wife Bonnie, from Mississippi, had spent a frustrating year there struggling to find meaningful work to support themselves. Bonnie's cousin, Margaret Dick, heard High Hawk speak in a church in Moun-tain Lake, Minnesota, in which he told the story of the Cheyenne's struggle to take over their schools. She told him about Dave. High

Hawk called and offered Dave the position as music teacher. Although they had no previous experience with Indian people, Dave and Bonnie accepted and moved to Busby.

In his teaching Dave used a tape recording of Cree and Eskimo songs, and parents soon asked, "Why not teach the children Cheyenne songs?" He responded, "You'll have to teach me first." So Corlette Teeth began teaching him. Then Gloria Big Back taught him the "Rabbit Song" and Lee Old Mouse began to teach him powwow songs. It was not long before Dave was accepted as one of the circle of drummers, providing the beat and leading the songs for social events at the school.

One day pastor Willis Busenitz from Busby took Dave along to a prayer meeting at Birney. There he heard Bear Sole lead Cheyenne Christians in singing their own songs of praise to God. Dave was fascinated. In church he had only heard the songs translated by missionaries from English or German and sung to the white man's music. I had been trying to record some of this indigenous music which was preserved mostly in the hearts and minds of Cheyenne Christians, especially in Oklahoma. Dave joined me on a trip there, and we were allowed to record many of these songs.

With the sponsorship of the Cheyenne Christian Education project (one of High Hawk's visions to help Cheyenne Christians walking the Jesus road), Dave edited *Tsese-Ma'heone-Nemeototse* (Cheyenne Spiritual Songs), a book of 161 songs with text and music. Ninety of

these songs, seen by Cheyenne Christians as "gifts of God the Creator," are in their own musical idiom. Red Medicine Woman leaves a legacy of praise to God in the 17 of her songs included in that hymn book.

Cheyenne spiritual songs.
(R. VOTH PHOTO)

High Hawk saw another need that the Cheyenne Christian Education project could help with. Most of the older Cheyenne Christians did not read in their own language. If they read some English, they found the Biblical language difficult to understand. Their contact with the Word was largely what they heard in church on Sundays. High Hawk wanted the scriptures to speak to them in their heart language.

A translation of the New Testament and portions of the Old Testament had been completed in 1934 by Rodolphe Petter with the help of Cheyenne Christians, but only a few Cheyennes really learned to read it well. Since that time new linguistic techniques had developed a more accurate alphabet for the Cheyenne language, and cassette players could make the word available to those who did not read. High Hawk's vision was that Cheyenne Christians themselves would do a fresh translation of Scriptures, a kind of "Today's Cheyenne Version." But he knew that they would need skilled help. "Where can we get a consultant who could work with us on such a project," he asked me.

I suggested that he contact Wycliffe Bible Translators who already had staff working with the neighboring Crow tribe. Wycliffe surveyed the situation and approved the project. It was Wayne Leman, son of an Alaskan fishing family, and his wife Elena, daughter of missionaries to Mexico, who felt God's urging to take up this task.

Red Medicine Woman gave an especially warm welcome to the Lemans. She adopted Wayne as her son, and helped him and his wife learn Cheyenne. Her attitude toward the Bible is revealed in the song in which she sings of *Ma'heo'o Tsene'taestse* (God the Lord). "Especially through his word I recognize him. I'll tell about him."[41]

Many Cheyenne Christians, too many to name here, have had a part in helping make the Word speak clearly and forcefully in Cheyenne. *Ota'taveennova'e* (Blue Feather Woman), who we know as Aline Killsontop, is giving much time to this task, and often reads

portions in church services. After one Sunday's reading, a Cheyenne
lady leaned over to her and said, "This is so right; if only people
would go by it." Aline says that hearing the Scriptures in Cheyenne
makes people feel like the elders are talking to them. People find it
difficult, she said, to understand the English Scriptures and yet are
often embarrassed to always ask to have them explained.[42]

A fresh translation into Cheyenne of Luke's Christmas and Easter
stories soon will be dubbed into an existing video which shows the
story of the gospel of Luke verse by verse. In this new way, Cheyenne
speakers will be able to hear the story of Jesus coming among us, the
peoples of this earth, in the language of their hearts.

You have come! And Red Medicine Woman responded to your
coming with this song:

> My heavenly Father
> I love you.
> I love you very much.
> I love you.[43]

Chapter 31

Joy Is Tan

What comes of Western shirts,
Prussian lace and beaded moccasins,
Ferns on high wooden pedestals,
Peyote buttons in low enamel pans,
Fry bread, and pluma moos, and potato chips,
Home-spun linen, Persian rugs, floors of earth,
Sage brush, rattlesnakes, peace roses in perfect rows,
Church bells with masses and church bells without,
Spirits, and science and predestination,
Branding irons, homemade sausage,
And Christmas trees from forests of pine?

It all comes in the package that I'm wrapped in,
Tied with the ribbon called love from the One who said,
"Let there be..." and there was.

A Time to Remember

Ann now views her experiences as a blend of the white and brown "worlds" in which she grew up. In her poem she ponders the vivid images she takes away from her years with us as a family living with the Cheyenne. The blending of white and brown have left their imprint on her life's journey.

And what of us, as we reflect on the involvement of our lives with those of the Cheyenne? How special it was for us to receive an

Ann

invitation to go back again to meet at Family Camp with our Cheyenne brothers and sisters! But was this the time? We hesitated at first when we thought through the schedule of July, the month we planned to retire after seven-and-a-half years of ministry with the Selkirk Christian Fellowship in Manitoba. Between Summer Bible School and last-minute requests for a baptism and a marriage, we were just too busy. "We'll come next year when we have more time," we said.

But that would not do. The surprise had to be spilled. Floyd Fisher wrote to the Selkirk Church stating that the focus of their family camp this year was to celebrate our 22 years of resident ministry among the Cheyenne plus 12 years of continuing visits for Indian Ministries. They wanted to give the Cheyenne version, a kind of "wrap-up" of those years. They offered to pay our expenses! They asked us to bring slides we had taken over the years.

Hot from an 800-mile drive from Selkirk, Manitoba, to Crazy Head Springs camp, we could hardly wait to taste the cold spring water. As we drove into camp, *Mata'ohnee'setse* (Gilbert Little Wolf), the camp leader, and Floyd Fisher, chairperson of the camp planning committee, both in jeans and western shirts, smiled broadly and gave us a casual but warm welcome. A banner reading "A Time to Remember" was hung on the side of the portable kitchen trailer. We soon had our tent up in the shade of the pines, and tired by the long drive, we went to our sleeping bags early.

The next morning familiar voices from Selkirk awakened us, and we discovered that a delegation of eight from Selkirk Christian Fellowship plus two friends from Winnipeg had followed us to Montana. Our family, we found out, had been invited as well, but of our five daughters only Rebecca, who as an adult had returned to the reservation to serve as a school nurse in Busby, was able to attend.

The first evening at the campfire, several young people whose parents and grandparents we'd known told about the recent changes in their lives that had brought them to this place.

Gilbert: "A few years ago I would not have stood up here. I didn't really know God. When I was drinking sometimes I couldn't remember. Today I get up in the morning and know what I am doing. All my family are sober except my adopted son."[44]

Mary Faye Eaglefeathers Bailey: "In 1971 I found the Lord, my life changed. I was like Gilbert, drinking. Now I have joy and peace. I wish everyone could have what I've found. It's so good. I'm thankful to the Lord for my new life."

Lenore Wolfname: "I often wondered what my grandfather [Davis Bailey] had. He walked to the Mennonite Church. He had something, but I didn't know what it was. Now I know. About a year ago I found the Lord too."

Floyd Fisher: "I used to bring my wife and her father up here and then I'd leave and go to [my home town of] Birney. I now have given my life to Jesus. I am happy to be here."

At the Saturday night campfire we looked at slides we had been taking ever since we bought our first camera in 1946. The pictures were projected onto a sheet hung between two pine trees. A gasoline-powered generator located over a hill to mute the noise provided electricity. Folks were excited to see pictures of parents, brothers or sisters no longer living, and together recalled the names of others. Little ones fell asleep on blankets near the fire as the remembering continued.

On Sunday morning, as High Hawk reminisced about our days with the Cheyenne, he chose to highlight the way we had encouraged Cheyenne Christians to make the decisions regarding the church. He

Bear Standing in the Shade and Walks On the Ground counting the offering.

remembered the time when his father, Bear Standing in the Shade, and his father's friend, Walks on the Ground, were given responsibility for the offerings. Each Sunday they recorded the amount with a short stubby pencil in a notebook kept in the church. They reported to the new church council. When the church needed coal, word got around, and we soon had collected enough to buy a truckload.

The churches gave retirement gifts. The Busby church gave us vests with Indian designs appliquéd on them. But they also gave us something else: warm hugs! Then Pastor Little Bear said to us, "Come over here and sit down. I never gave an order like that to you before!" We sat down in the folding lawn chairs, "powwow chairs," the Cheyenne call them. Jason White Man was standing near him with a brown paper bag holding the presents.

But before he gave us the presents, Little Bear told stories about our ministries. "When I became pastor of the Lame Deer Mennonite Church there was a Cheyenne man who was giving me a bad time," he said. "Whenever he saw me in public he would ridicule me. It got so that I couldn't take it anymore. I was going to talk it over with

Malcolm but he wasn't at home. So I talked it over with Esther. I told her about the harassment this man was giving me. Esther listened, discussed it, and finally said, 'Joe, let's pray that the God's Holy Spirit will be at work. Who knows, maybe someday God will turn this around for His glory.' We prayed."

"Sometime later," Joe continued, "I saw this man shoving people aside and coming right toward me. Then I noticed he was crying. He told me that he had backed his pickup over his son and killed him. He wanted me to lead the funeral." Then Joe got down on his knees, took off our shoes, and replaced them with some gorgeous beaded moccasins. I thought of Jesus washing the disciples' feet.

The Ashland Mennonite Church gave us beautiful beaded necklaces, and then hugs too! The hugs we received on this occasion surprised us. Although we had seen Cheyenne Christians hugging each other, being hugged was a first-time experience for us.

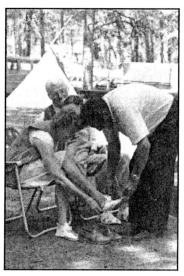

Pastor Little Bear giving Malcolm and Esther moccasins.

We received other gifts. Gilbert Little Wolf lined up his family, including children and grandchildren. We were expected to shake hands with each one, thanking them for the gift. As a part of his handshake Gilbert pressed some bills into my hand. *Vonahe'e* (Elizabeth Risingsun), struggling with illness, sent her daughter Louise Fisher to Hardin to purchase a treasured Pendelton blanket. Though she was not well enough to be there, we felt her presence in the blanket with which her daughter honored us.

Malcolm
(JOHN SCHMIDT PHOTO, 1953)

These wonderful days at Family Camp helped us to think back over our years with the Cheyenne. I remembered the time when I was about ready to quit after a few years at Busby. If we were going to continue to import leaders on into the future, I did not want to be a part of it. How would we know when our missionary work would be finished? It was already more than 40 years old.

I stumbled across a booklet with the somewhat clumsy title, *Reaching the Last Tribe in this Generation via Indigenous New Testament Methods.*[45] I learned some valuable lessons from it about our mission work, but more important, I was led on to the classic on the subject, Rowland Allen's *Missionary Methods: St. Paul's or Ours?*[46] In it, this Anglican missionary to China contrasted the New Testament record of Paul's way of doing missions with ours. I began to see that the development of a responsible church, able to manage its own affairs, was the answer to my question about how we would know when our work was done.

I had said publicly to the Christians at Busby that we would not always be there and that that was why we were shaping the church to get along without us. "We would be like orphans," objected White Blanket (Davis Bailey). He promptly started attending the only other church then in the community (Catholic). But soon he returned to the White River Cheyenne Mennonite Church.

On one of my visits back to Busby the congregation was struggling with the question of calling a new pastor. Some in the congregation were interested in a non-Indian Christian living in Lame Deer.

I suggested that the congregation might want to use the resources of the conference personnel office to gather the opinions of people who knew the candidate better than we did.

The report of the personnel office had raised serious cautions about the couple. When I shared the negative information, one woman said, "I thought you said that *we* were going to make the decision." "That's right," I said, "the decision is yours." The church decided to extend a call to this couple.

Some time later, a neighbor's quarter horse came through a broken fence and rubbed against the wall of the new pastor's house. Instead of fixing the fence, the pastor got mad, and lamed the horse with a shotgun blast. This was an almost unforgivable sin in horse country. But the church stood by him. After all, they had chosen him despite warnings that there were problems. The pastor and his wife chose to leave the area. The next time a pastor was called, the church accepted counsel.

As Indian Christian leaders now take much more responsibility for the decisions affecting the life of the church, some of them are also beginning to experiment with Indian forms of worship. The pastoral couple (Crow/Cheyenne) that led a communion service at the Mennonite Indian Leaders Council meeting some years ago offered a Cheyenne symbol of cleansing (the smoke of sage leaves on hot coals) as an optional preparation for taking communion. Some of the native Christians were very uncomfortable with this, commenting, "I thought that we left all that behind when we became Christians." I was reminded of a similar response of some Christians when they learned that Cheyenne Christians were using traditional melodies in praise of Jesus.

At a recent inter-tribal and inter-Mennonite Assembly of First Nation Christians, Steve Cheramie Risingsun, a Houma leader from Mississippi, ventured some guidelines for what he describes as an "enculturated" church. "Every culture has ways that they welcome infants into society, give them names, celebrate the first smile or first step, conduct marriages and burials. There is a need to teach people how to take these traditions and bring them to Christ. Such cultural forms if consistent with the Christian ethic may be used in the church. If at odds with the Christian ethic the church should substitute its own form to meet the cultural need."

There are still many unanswered questions as to how one can be truly Indian and truly Christian at the same time. These are questions that native Christians will need to answer from their knowledge of their own tribes' culture and with the guidance of the Holy Spirit and the Word of God. These are questions that outsiders are often poorly equipped to answer.

Through our contacts with the Cheyenne people these many years, we have become more willing to listen to others—to respect the views of those who differ from us. We have come to see the Christian message as an invitation, supported by loving service, rather than a new ideology that could be forced on another people by a more powerful culture.

We experienced the honesty with which Cheyenne people shared the darker experiences of life. In our own culture, we found that people often preferred to wear masks, to conceal the failures and rough places in life. We decided that the "civilization" we had unthinkingly tried so hard to sell along with Christianity was sometimes more savage than we had been willing to admit. The civilization Native peoples had experienced had damaged and besmirched the Good News we were sent to share.

It is God's love that through us, and at times in spite of us, draws people of all cultures to Jesus and closer to each other. God's love provides healing for the wounds of life that native peoples have suffered in greater than equal share. We are glad that we could have a small part in bringing the message of God's healing and hope to the Cheyenne people.

Notes

1 David Graber, compiler and music editor, *Tsese-Ma'heone-Nemeototse: Cheyenne Spiritual Songs* (Newton, KS: Faith and Life Press, 1982), No. 55.

2 Scripture quotations (unless otherwise noted) are from the *Holy Bible*, New International Version (Grand Rapids, MI: Zondervan Bible Publishers, 1994).

3 Tom Weist, *A History of the Cheyenne People* (Billings, MT: Montana Council for Indian Education, 1977), p. 123.

4 Ibid., p. 124.

5 Ibid., p. 114.

6 E. Douglas Branch, *The Hunting of the Buffalo* (Lincoln: University of Nebraska Press, 1962), p. xxxii.

7 Ibid., pp. 224-227.

8 Ibid., pp. 222-223.

9 Ibid., p. 232.

10 Weist, pp. 112, 114.

11 Ibid., pp. 188, 189.

[12]   George Bird Grinnel, *The Cheyenne Indians: Their History and Their Way of Life*, 2 vols. (New York: Cooper Square Publishers, 1923, reprinted 1982), vol. 2, p. 161.

[13]   John Woodenlegs, *The Native American Church* (Busby, MT: The Busby School, audio tape, n.d.).

[14]   *Amended Articles of Incorporation of the Native American Church of the United States* (El Reno, Oklahoma, June 4, 1944).

[15]   Woodenlegs.

[16]   Robert M. Utley, *Frontier Regulars: The United States Army and the Indian, 1866-1890* (New York: Macmillan Publishing Co., 1973), p. 263.

[17]   Ibid., pp. 277, 278.

[18]   This story is told in detail by Mari Sandoz in *Cheyenne Autumn* (New York: McGraw Hill, 1963).

[19]   *Cheyenne Spiritual Songs*, No. 8.

[20]   John Stands In Timber and Margot Liberty, *Cheyenne Memories* (New Haven and London: Yale University Press, 1967), p. 292.

[21]   Grinnell, *Cheyenne Indians*, vol. 1, p.156.

[22]   Elvis Presley, "Hound Dog," in *First Time Ever: 650 Outstanding Songs*, Dutchess Music Corporation and Soldier Music, Los Angeles, California (Melville, NY: MCA/Mills Joint Venture, 1972), page 258.

23   For further understanding of the role of unresolved grief in addiction, see Arthur H., *The Grieving Indian, An Ojibwe Elder Shares His Discovery of Help and Hope* (Winnipeg, Manitoba: Indian Life Books, 1988).

24   *Cheyenne Spiritual Songs*, No. 99.

25   George Bird Grinnell, *By Cheyenne Campfires* (New Haven: Yale University Press, 1926), pp. 182-193.

26   Don Richardson, *Peace Child* (Glendale California: Regal Books, 1974). See especially chapters 17-19, pp.193-231.

27   Ibid., p. 288.

28   Christopher Columbus, *The Log of Christopher Columbus*, translated by Robert H. Fuson (Camden, ME: International Marine Publishing Company, 1987), p. 51.

29   Howard Zinn, *A People's History of the United States* (New York: Harper Collins, 1980), p.3.

30   Ibid., pp. 4, 5.

31   Stan Hoig, *The Peace Chiefs of the Cheyennes* (Norman, OK: University of Oklahoma Press, 1980), p. 7.

32   Dee Brown, *Bury My Heart at Wounded Knee: An Indian History of the American West* (New York: Bantam Books, 1970), p. 70.

33   Ibid., Chapter 4.

34   Ibid., pp. 162-164.

35   *The Teachable Moment, A Christian Response to the Native Peoples of the Americas* (Mennonite Central Committee, Canada, 1992), p. 27.

36   Arthur H., pp. 18, 19, 23-27.

37   Henri J. M. Nouwen, *The Wounded Healer* (Garden City, NY: Image Books, 1979).

38   David Augsburger, *Caring Enough Not to Forgive/Caring Enough to Forgive* (Gospel Light Publishers, 1981).

39   *Cheyenne Spiritual Songs*, No. 30.

40   Maude Fightingbear, "How I Received My Songs," in *Naevhoo'ohtseme/We Are Going Home: Cheyenne History and Stories Told by James Shoulderblade and Others* (Winnipeg, Manitoba: Algonquian and Iriquoian Linguistics, 1987), pp. 152-169.

41   *Cheyenne Spiritual Songs*, No. 100.

42   Elena Leman, letter, July 10, 1998.

43   *Cheyenne Spiritual Songs*, No. 81.

44   This and the following three testimonies are from notes Esther Wenger took at the occasion.

45   William S. Dillon, *Reaching the Last Tribe in this Generation via the Indigenous New Testament Methods* (New Tribes Mission, 871 Rush Street, Chicago, Illinois, 1945).

46   Roland Allen, *Missionary Methods: St. Paul's or Ours?* (Grand Rapids, MI: Wm. B. Erdmans Publishing Co., 1962, reprinted in 1989). My first copy of this book came from World Dominion Press, London, England. Not many books first printed in 1912 are still in demand as this one is.

Acknowledgments

This book has been a family project. It started with Ann, who dealt with the aftermath of trauma by writing the poems that appear here. She, in turn, invited her parents to give context to the poetry by telling how they experienced and thought about the events that it describes. She also did the artwork for the cover and kept patiently encouraging us. Martha, with her experience in editing, spent many hours improving the text. Grace and Rebecca helped choose the photos. They and Elizabeth kept cheering us on, and offered to help with the expense of publishing.

We owe much to the *Tsetsastase*, the Cheyenne people, who became our friends, and from whom we learned so much. We are also indebted to the First Nation and Metis people of Canada, who stretched us to adapt to new cultures. Thanks also to the individuals who gave us permission to tell their stories, to Louise and Floyd Fisher who read the book and gave us valuable guidance; and to Joe and Victoria Walks Along, who also read drafts of some of the book and suggested corrections.

Wayne Leman, of Wycliffe Bible Translators, and Louise Fisher both gave us invaluable help in checking our use of Cheyenne names and words. (A new and more accurate alphabet has been developed since our days with the Cheyenne.) Chris Graber, staff person for the Mennonite Indian Leaders Council, and Lois Barrett, Secretary of the Commission on Home Ministries of the General Conference Mennonite Church, encouraged us and helped us publish this book. Thanks is due to them all.

About Pandora Press

Pandora Press is a small, independently owned press dedicated to making available modestly priced books that deal with Anabaptist, Mennonite, and Believers Church topics, both historical and theological. We welcome comments from our readers.

Visit our full-service online Bookstore:
www.pandorapress.com

Esther and Malcom Wenger, poetry by Ann Wenger, *Healing the Wounds* (Kitchener: Pandora Press, 2001; co-published with Herald Press).
   Softcover, 210 pp. ISBN 1-894710-09-6.
   $18.50 US/$21.00 Canadian. Postage: $5.00 US/$7.00 Can.
[**Experiences of Mennonite missionaries with the Cheyenne**]

Pedro A. Sandín-Fremaint, *Cuentos y Encuentros: Hacia una Educación Transformadora* (Kitchener: Pandora Press, 2001).
   Softcover 163 pp ISBN 1-894710-08-8.
   $12.00 US/ $16.00 Canadian. Postage $5.00 US/$7.00 Canadian.
[**Spanish. Stories/ discussion questions for Christian education**]

A. James Reimer, *Mennonites and Classical Theology: Dogmatic Foundations for Christian Ethics* (Kitchener: Pandora Press, 2001; co-published with Herald Press)
   Softcover, 650pp. ISBN 0-9685543 7 7
   $52.00 U.S./$65.00 Canadian. Postage: $5.00 U.S./$7.00 Can.
[**A theological interpretation of Mennonite experience in 20th C.**]

Walter Klaassen, *Anabaptism: Neither Catholic nor Protestant*, 3rd ed (Kitchener: Pandora Press, 2001; co-pub. Herald Press)
   Softcover, 122pp. ISBN 1-894710-01-0
   $12.00 U.S./$15.00 Can. Postage: $3.00 U.S./$4.00 Can.
[**A classic interpretation and study guide, now available again**]

Dale Schrag & James Juhnke, eds., *Anabaptist Visions for the new Millennium: A search for identity* (Kitchener: Pandora Press, 2001; co-published with Herald Press)

Softcover, 242 pp. ISBN 1-894710-00-2

$18.00 U.S./$24.00 Canadian. Postage $4.00 U.S./$5.00 Can.

[Twenty-eight essays presented at Bethel College, June, 2000]

Harry Loewen, ed., *Road to Freedom: Mennonites Escape the Land of Suffering* (Kitchener: Pandora Press, 2000; co-published with Herald Press)

Hardcover, large format, 302pp. ISBN 0-9685543-5-0

$35.00 U.S./$39.50 Canadian. Postage: $7.00 U.S./$8.00 Can.

[Life experiences documented with personal stories and photos]

Alan Kreider and Stuart Murray, eds., *Coming Home: Stories of Anabaptists in Britain and Ireland* (Kitchener: Pandora Press, 2000; co-published with Herald Press)

Softcover, 220pp. ISBN 0-9685543-6-9

$22.00 U.S./$25.00 Canadian. Postage: $4.00 U.S./$5.00 Can.

[Anabaptist encounters in the U.K.; personal stories/articles]

Edna Schroeder Thiessen and Angela Showalter, *A Life Displaced: A Mennonite Woman's Flight from War-Torn Poland* (Kitchener: Pandora Press, 2000; co-published with Herald Press)

Softcover, xii, 218pp. ISBN 0-9685543-2-6

$20.00 U.S./$24.00 Canadian. Postage: $4.00 U.S./$5.00 Can.

[A true story: moving, richly-detailed, told with candor and courage]

Stuart Murray, *Biblical Interpretation in the Anabaptist Tradition* (Kitchener: Pandora Press, 2000; co-published with Herald Press)

Softcover, 310pp. ISBN 0-9685543-3-4

$28.00 U.S./$32.00 Canadian. Postage: $4.00 U.S./$5.00 Can.

[How Anabaptists read the Bible; considerations for today's church]

Apocalypticism and Millennialism, ed. by Loren L. Johns
(Kitchener: Pandora Press, 2000; co-published with Herald Press)
    Softcover, 419pp; Scripture and name indeces
    ISBN 0-9683462-9-4
    $37.50 U.S./$44.00 Canadian. Postage: $5.00 U.S./$6.00 Can.
[A clear, careful, and balanced collection: pastoral and scholarly]

Later Writings by Pilgram Marpeck and his Circle. Volume 1: *The
Exposé, A Dialogue and Marpeck's Response to Caspar Schwenckfeld*
Translated by Walter Klaassen, Werner Packull, and John Rempel
(Kitchener: Pandora Press, 1999; co-published with Herald Press)
    Softcover, 157pp. ISBN 0-9683462-6-X
    $20.00 U.S./$23.00 Canadian. Postage: $4.00 U.S./$5.00 Can.
[Previously untranslated writings by Marpeck and his Circle]

John Driver, *Radical Faith. An Alternative History of the
Christian Church,* edited by Carrie Snyder.
(Kitchener: Pandora Press, 1999; co-published with Herald Press)
    Softcover, 334pp. ISBN 0-9683462-8-6
    $32.00 U.S./$35.00 Canadian. Postage: $5.00 U.S./$6.00 Can.
[A history of the church as it is seldom told – from the margins]

C. Arnold Snyder, *From Anabaptist Seed. The Historical Core of
Anabaptist-Related Identity*
(Kitchener: Pandora Press, 1999; co-published with Herald Press)
    Softcover, 53pp.; discussion questions. ISBN 0-9685543-0-X
    $5.00 U.S./$6.25 Canadian. Postage: $2.00 U.S./$2.50 Can.
[Ideal for group study, commissioned by Mennonite World Conf.]
Also available in Spanish translation: *De Semilla Anabautista,*
from Pandora Press only.

John D. Thiesen, *Mennonite and Nazi? Attitudes Among
Mennonite Colonists in Latin America, 1933-1945.*
(Kitchener: Pandora Press, 1999; co-published with Herald Press)
    Softcover, 330pp., 2 maps, 24 b/w illustrations, bibliography,
    index. ISBN 0-9683462-5-1
    $25.00 U.S./$28.00 Canadian. Postage: $4.00 U.S./$5.00 Can.
[Careful and objective study of an explosive topic]

Lifting the Veil, a translation of *Aus meinem Leben: Erinnerungen von J.H. Janzen.* Ed. by Leonard Friesen; trans. by Walter Klaassen (Kitchener: Pandora Press, 1998; co-pub. with Herald Press).
   Softcover, 128pp.; 4pp. of illustrations. ISBN 0-9683462-1-9
   $12.50 U.S./$14.00 Canadian. Postage: $4.00 U.S. and Can.
[Memoir, confession, critical observation of Mennonite life in Russia]

Leonard Gross, *The Golden Years of the Hutterites*, rev. ed.
(Kitchener: Pandora Press, 1998; co-pub. with Herald Press).
   Softcover, 280pp., index. ISBN 0-9683462-3-5
   $22.00 U.S./$25.00 Canadian. Postage: $4.00 U.S./$5.00 Can.
[Classic study of early Hutterite movement, now available again]

The Believers Church: A Voluntary Church, ed. by William H. Brackney (Kitchener: Pandora Press, 1998; co-published with Herald Press).
   Softcover, viii, 237pp., index. ISBN 0-9683462-0-0
   $25.00 U.S./$27.50 Canadian. Postage: $4.00 U.S./$5.00 Can.
[Papers from the 12th Believers Church Conference, Hamilton, ON]

An Annotated Hutterite Bibliography, compiled by Maria H. Krisztinkovich, ed. by Peter C. Erb (Kitchener, Ont.: Pandora Press, 1998). (Ca. 2,700 entries) 312pp., cerlox bound, electronic, or both.
   ISBN (paper) 0-9698762-8-9/(disk) 0-9698762-9-7
   $15.00 each, U.S. and Canadian. Postage: $6.00 U.S. and Can.
[The most extensive bibliography on Hutterite literature available]

Jacobus ten Doornkaat Koolman, *Dirk Philips. Friend and Colleague of Menno Simons*, trans. W. E. Keeney, ed. C. A. Snyder (Kitchener: Pandora Press, 1998; co-pub. with Herald Press).
   Softcover, xviii, 236pp., index. ISBN: 0-9698762-3-8
   $23.50 U.S./$28.50 Canadian. Postage: $4.00 U.S./$5.00 Can.
[The definitive biography of Dirk Philips, now available in English]

Sarah Dyck, ed./tr., *The Silence Echoes: Memoirs of Trauma & Tears* (Kitchener: Pandora Press, 1997; co-published with Herald Press). Softcover, xii, 236pp., 2 maps. ISBN: 0-9698762-7-0 $17.50 U.S./$19.50 Canadian. Postage: $4.00 U.S./$5.00 Can. [First person accounts of life in the Soviet Union, trans. from German]

Wes Harrison, *Andreas Ehrenpreis and Hutterite Faith and Practice* (Kitchener: Pandora Press, 1997; co-published with Herald Press). Softcover, xxiv, 274pp., 2 maps, index. ISBN 0-9698762-6-2 $26.50 U.S./$32.00 Canadian. Postage: $4.00 U.S./$5.00 Can. [First biography of this important seventeenth century Hutterite leader]

C. Arnold Snyder, *Anabaptist History and Theology: Revised Student Edition* (Kitchener: Pandora Press, 1997; co-pub. Herald Press). Softcover, xiv, 466pp., 7 maps, 28 illustrations, index, bibliography. ISBN 0-9698762-5-4 $35.00 U.S./$38.00 Canadian. Postage: $5.00 U.S./$6.00 Can. [Abridged, rewritten edition for undergraduates and the non-specialist]

Nancey Murphy, *Reconciling Theology and Science: A Radical Reformation Perspective* (Kitchener, Ont.: Pandora Press, 1997; co-pub. Herald Press). Softcover, x, 103pp., index. ISBN 0-9698762-4-6 $14.50 U.S./$17.50 Canadian. Postage: $3.50 U.S./$4.00 Can. [Exploration of the supposed conflict between Christianity and Science]

C. Arnold Snyder and Linda A. Huebert Hecht, eds, *Profiles of Anabaptist Women: Sixteenth Century Reforming Pioneers* (Waterloo, Ont.: Wilfrid Laurier University Press, 1996). Softcover, xxii, 442pp. ISBN: 0-88920-277-X $28.95 U.S. or Canadian. Postage: $5.00 U.S./$6.00 Can. [Biographical sketches of more than 50 Anabaptist women; a first]

The Limits of Perfection: A Conversation with J. Lawrence Burkholder 2nd ed., with a new epilogue by J. Lawrence Burkholder, Rodney Sawatsky and Scott Holland, eds.
(Kitchener: Pandora Press, 1996).
   Softcover, x, 154pp. ISBN 0-9698762-2-X
   $10.00 U.S./$13.00 Canadian. Postage: $2.00 U.S./$3.00 Can.
[J.L. Burkholder on his life experiences; eight Mennonites respond]

C. Arnold Snyder, *Anabaptist History and Theology: An Introduction* (Kitchener: Pandora Press, 1995).
   ISBN 0-9698762-0-3 Softcover, x, 434pp., 6 maps,
   29 illustrations, index, bibliography.
   $35.00 U.S./$38.00 Canadian. Postage: $5.00 U.S./$6.00 Can.
[Comprehensive survey; unabridged version, fully documented]

C. Arnold Snyder, *The Life and Thought of Michael Sattler* (Scottdale: Herald Press, 1984).
   Hardcover, viii, 260pp. ISBN 0-8361-1264-4
   $10.00 U.S./$12.00 Canadian. Postage: $4.00 U.S./$5.00 Can.
[First full-length biography of this Anabaptist leader and martyr]

Pandora Press
51 Pandora Avenue N.
Kitchener, Ontario
Canada N2H 3C1
Tel./Fax: (519) 578-2381
E-mail:
info@pandorapress.com
Web site:
www.pandorapress.com

Herald Press
616 Walnut Avenue
Scottdale, PA
U.S.A. 15683
Orders: (800) 245-7894
E-mail:
hp@mph.org
Web site:
www.mph.org